THE SCRIPTURES
THE ONLY
RULE OF FAITH:

AN EXPOSITION
OF THE
SECOND ANSWER
OF THE SHORTER CATECHISM

BY THE

REV. JOHN HALL
PASTOR OF THE PRESBYTERIAN CHURCH, TRENTON, NJ

SOLID GROUND CHRISTIAN BOOKS
PORT ST LUCIE, FL USA

SOLID GROUND CHRISTIAN BOOKS
1682 SW Pancoast Street
Port St Lucie FL 34987
(205) 587-4480
mike.sgcb@gmail.com
http://www.solid-ground-books.com

THE SCRIPTURES: The Only Rule of Faith
An Exposition of the 2nd Answer of the Shorter Catechism

by John Hall (1806-1894)

FIRST SOLID GROUND EDITION – July 2019

Taken from the 1844 Edition

Cover Design by Borgo Design, Tuscaloosa, Alabama

ISBN: 978-159925-398-5

TABLE OF CONTENTS

CHAPTER I	
A Rule	9
CHAPTER II	
God's Rule	13
CHAPTER III	
The Word of God is Contained in the Scriptures	17
CHAPTER IV	
The Holy Scriptures are Their Own Witness	25
CHAPTER V	
The Word of God Directs us	32
CHAPTER VI	
How the Scriptures Direct us	39
CHAPTER VII	
The Scriptures are the Only Rule	49
CHAPTER VIII	
The Scriptures Show that they are the Only Rule	54
CHAPTER IX	
The Scriptures Warn us Against Other Rules	57
CHAPTER X	
Other Rules; --the Apocrypha	61
CHAPTER XI	
Other Rules;--the Koran, the Shastres, Swendenborg's Books, &c,	67
CHAPTER XII	
Other Rules;--Inward Light, Human Reason, &c.,	74
CHAPTER XIII	
Other Rules; --Tradition	78
CHAPTER XIV	
Tradition Continued;--The Church Fathers	85
CHAPTER XV	
Tradition Continued;--The Church	90
CHAPTER XVI	
Conclusion	97

PREFACE

There is evidently a peculiar necessity at the present time for encouraging the study of the Scriptures, and for maintaining their sole and independent authority as the rule of faith and conduct. Our children are accustomed to learn the truth on this subject, at their second step in the Catechism, and they afterwards find the same doctrine more fully opened, in the first chapter of our Confession of Faith. But the proofs need to be familiarly stated and illustrated, in order to give this fundamental principle its proper place in the mind. This is the main design of the exposition now offered. It is hoped that it may prove useful to young persons generally; and that it may be added to the few manuals prepared with a special view to families, Bible classes, and Sabbath schools, connected with the Presbyterian Church.

John Hall
Trenton, New Jersey

INTRODUCTION*
by John Whitecross

The following illustrations are given to open up the answer to Question Two of The Shorter Catechism: "The Word of God, which is contained in the Scriptures of the Old and New Testaments, is the only rule to direct us how we may glorify and enjoy Him."

1. A gentleman, travelling in a stagecoach, attempted to divert the company by ridiculing the Scriptures. 'As to the prophecies,' said he, 'in particular, they were all written after the events took place.' A minister in the coach, who had hitherto been silent, replied, 'Sir, I beg leave to mention one particular prophecy as an exception, 2 Pet. 3. 3, "Knowing this first, that there shall come in the last days *scoffers."* Now, sir, whether the event be not long after the prediction, I leave the company to judge.' The mouth of the scorner was stopped.

2. When the famous Duke of Wellington was, in the early part of his career—he was then Sir Arthur Wellesley—stationed in India, an officer, dining at the mess where he presided, was sporting his infidel sentiments. Sir Arthur wishing to put down such conversation, said, S , did you ever read Paley's Evidences? The reply was in the negative. 'Well then,' 'aid Sir Arthur, 'you had better read that book before you talk in the way you are doing.' The occurrence passed away, and the conversation was soon forgotten; but the reference to Paley's work led Colonel S. to inquire after it, and having obtained a copy, he read it with the most serious attention. He rose from the perusal of it with the fullest conviction of the falsehood of the system he had formerly adopted, and of the divine origin of Christianity. But he did not stop here, he was determined to examine the Book itself, which he was thus satisfied was a revelation from God. The result was, that he cordially received this revelation of mercy, saw and felt his need of a Savior, and believing in Jesus, became a Christian, not in name only, but in deed and in truth. Colonel S. feeling his obligation to Sir Arthur, after-wards wrote to him, thanking him for his kindness, in recommending to him Dr Paley's valuable work; and earnestly advising him not to be satisfied with merely knowing the external evidence of Christianity, but to inquire what this divine communication really contains. It is not known whether any reply was made to this communication.

3. Naimbanna, a black prince from the neighborhood of Sierra Leone, arrived in England in 1791. The gentleman to whose care he was entrusted, took great pains to convince him that the Bible was the Word of God, and he received it as such, with great reverence and simplicity. Do we ask what it was that satisfied him on this subject? Let us listen to his artless words. 'When I found,' said he, 'all good men minding the Bible, and calling it the Word of God, and all bad men disregarding it, I then was sure that the Bible must be what good men called it, the Word of God.'

4. 'A few Sabbaths ago,' says one, 'a little boy, about six years of age, just after entering the school, came and asked me for the charity-box. I inquired what he wanted with it. "I want to put a halfpenny into it," said he. To examine his motives, and his knowledge of divine things more particularly, I asked him what good he supposed it would do to put his money into the charity-box. "I want to send it to the heathen," he replied. "Do you know," said I, "who the heathen are?" "They are folks who have not got any Bible, and live a great way *off.*" "What is the Bible?" "The Word of God." "Of what use would it be to the heathen, if they had it?" "It would tell them to love God, and be good." "Where did the Bible come from?" "From heaven." "Was it written in heaven?" "No, the prophets and good men wrote it." "If good men wrote it, how then is it the Word of God, and came from heaven?" "Why, the Holy Ghost told them how to write it." "Did they see the Holy Ghost, and did He speak to them?" "No, but He made them *think* it." This was enough. I presented to him the charity-box; he dropped in his money; a smile of joy glowed upon his countenance; and he returned to his seat filled with the luxury of doing good.'

5. The learned Salmasius of Burgundy said on his death-bed, 'O! I have lost a world of time! If one year more were added to my life, it should be spent in reading David's Psalms, and Paul's Epistles.'

6. John Locke, a little before his death, being asked what was the shortest and surest way for a young gentleman to attain a true knowledge of the Christian religion, made this reply; 'Let him study the Holy Scriptures, especially the New Testament; therein are contained the words of eternal life. It has God for its author, salvation for its end, and truth, without any mixture of error, for its matter.'

7. It was customary, in Cromwell's time, for his soldiers to carry each a Bible in his pocket; among others, a profligate young man, who was ordered out to attack some fortress. During the engagement, a bullet had perforated his Bible, and gone so far as to rest opposite these words in Ecclesiastes; 'Rejoice, O young man, in thy youth, and let thy heart cheer thee in the days of thy youth; and walk in the ways of thy heart, and in the

sight of thine eyes: but know thou, that for all these things God will bring thee into judgment.' These words so appropriate to his case, powerfully affected his mind, and proved, by the blessing of God, the means of his conversion. He used to observe that the Bible had been the happy means of saving both his soul and his body.

8. During days of war a godly man visited a camp of French soldiers at Toulon, taking with him a number of French New Testaments which he distributed to the men, many of whom seemed pleased with the gift. He had at length exhausted all his store, with the exception of one copy; this he offered to a man standing near him. The man took it, opened it, and turning to a companion said sneeringly, 'Oh, this will do to light my pipe with.' A discouraging enough reception; but the book, having been once given, was beyond recovery.

About a year and half after this occurrence, the distributor of the Testaments was on a short journey through the South of France and stopped on his way at a roadside inn for refreshment and a night's lodging. On entering the house, he soon perceived that something of a sad nature had happened to the landlady. On inquiring what it was, she informed him that her eldest son had been buried that very week. She went on very naturally to dilate on his many excellencies and spoke of his happy deathbed. 'And sir,' said she, 'all his happiness was got from a little book that was given him sometime ago.' The traveler inquired further concerning the little book. 'You shall see it,' said the mother, 'it is upstairs.' She soon returned with the book. On opening it, he found it to be French New Testament, and identified it as the very one he had himself given, so many months before, to that seemingly unpromising soldier at Toulon. He discovered that five or six of the early pages had been torn out, thus indicating that the man had actually commenced the fulfilment of his threat to use the book to light his pipe with. This was not all. On the inside cover were written the words: 'Given to me at Toulon on —day; first despised, then read, and finally blessed to the saving of my soul.'

9. Two men came one night to a missionary in Madagascar. They had walked a hundred miles out of their way to visit him. 'Have you the Bible?' asked the missionary. 'We have seen it and heard it read,' one man said, 'but we have only some of the words of David, and they do not belong to us; they belong to the whole family.' 'Have you the words of David with you now?' asked the missionary. They looked at each other but would not answer. Perhaps they were afraid, but the kindness of the speaker moved one of the men to put his hand into his bosom and to take out what seemed to be a roll of cloth. He unrolled it and, after the removal of a few wrappers, there appeared a few old, torn, dingy leaves of the Psalms which had been

read, passed round, lent and re-read, until they were almost worn out. Tears came into the missionary's eyes when he saw them. 'Have you ever seen the words of the Lord Jesus, or John or Paul or Peter?' he asked. 'Yes, they said, 'we have seen and heard them, but we never owned them.' The missionary then brought out a Testament with the Book of Psalms bound up with it and showed it to them. 'Now,' said he, 'if you will give me your few words of David, I will give you all his words, and all the words of the Lord Jesus, and John and Paul and Peter besides.' The men were amazed and delighted. But they wanted to see if the words of David were the same in the missionary's book, and when they found that they were, and thousands more of the same sort, their joy knew no bounds. They willingly gave up their poor, tattered leaves, seized the volume, thanked the missionary, bade him good-bye, and started off upon their long journey home, rejoicing like those who had found a great spoil.

10. A peasant in the county of Cork, understanding that a gentleman had a copy of the Scriptures in the Irish language, begged permission to see it. He asked whether he might borrow the New Testament in his own tongue that he might make a copy of it. The gentleman said that he could not obtain another copy, and that he was afraid to trust it with him so that he might take a copy in writing. 'Where will you get the paper?' he asked. 'I will buy it.' 'And the pens and ink?' 'I will buy them.' 'Where will you find a place to do the work?' 'If your honor will allow me your hall, I will come after I have done my work in the day and take a copy by portions of time in the evening.' The owner of the book was so struck with his zeal that he gave him the use of the hall and a light, in order to make the copy. The man was firm to his purpose, in course of time finished the work, and produced a copy of the New Testament in writing by his own hand. A printed copy was later given him in exchange for it, and the written one was placed in the hands of the President of a Bible Society as a monument of the desire of the Irish to know the Scriptures.

*taken from the book *The Shorter Catechism Illustrated* published by Solid Ground Christian Books

THE ONLY RULE OF FAITH.

CHAPTER I.

A RULE.

I MUST begin this book by supposing that every one who shall undertake to read it, knows the meaning of the answer to the first question in the Shorter Catechism; namely, that "Man's Chief End is to glorify God and to enjoy Him forever."

As soon as this is understood and believed, it is natural to ask, How can we do it? For, surely, we may expect, that even a child, when convinced that he was created and is kept in life, for one principal purpose, will be anxious to learn the way in which that purpose can be accomplished. He will then feel the need of something to guide him; to show him what he has to do, and how he is to do it. In other words, he needs *a rule to direct him.*

This is the shortest explanation of what a rule is. It is that which directs us how to do a certain thing. The direction may be given in different ways, according to the nature of the thing to be done, but in every case that which directs is the rule. When you copy a picture, or write in a copy-book, the picture or written pattern is the rule to direct you. The paper on which you write is said to be *ruled*, because the lines direct you how to write evenly. The carpenter has an instrument, called a rule, which directs him, as a measure and as a straight line, in the size and proportions of what he makes: as the prophet Isaiah, describing how an image is made of a block of wood for an idol, says, "the carpenter stretcheth out his rule; he marketh it out with a line; he fitteth it with planes, and he marketh it out with the compass, and maketh it after the figure of a man." (Isaiah xliv. 13.)

All rules of the kind just mentioned may be called mechanical. They direct us how to perform things which are done with our hands. They have not so much to do with our minds, and nothing with our hearts, or with teaching us what is good and evil.

There are other rules which our minds alone can follow, and neither our hands nor hearts have any thing to do with them. Such are those parts of grammar which are called rules, because they direct us how to speak correctly; or the rules of arithmetic which instruct us how to calculate.

Then there are rules which govern our conduct in different situations; as the rules of a school, or of a family; and a school or family not governed in this way would be called irregular or unregulated, which words mean to be without rules.

Again, there are rules to direct our conduct as citizens. These are commonly called laws, and are the rule of civil conduct; that is, they regulate our conduct as citizens, by directing us to do certain things, and to avoid doing others. It is on this account that those who are appointed to see that the laws are observed, are called rulers; and the Scriptures apply that name also to the heads of families and to the officers of churches, all of whom are required to "rule well." (1 Tim. iii. 4. v. 17.)

Before I proceed to speak of the highest kind of rule, I wish you to notice, that however different from one another those are that have been mentioned, there are some points in which they are alike.

For example; whether we copy from a pattern, or write with the help of lines, or make some article with tools, or speak grammatically, or obey the laws, in all these cases the rule which directs us is,

I. Something that is fixed and certain. We can see, or hear, or read it, and know exactly what we have to do.

II. It must be strictly followed, if we would do what is required in each case.

III. We do not follow the rule as we follow advice or persuasion, or our own choice only; but we are bound to follow it as a matter of obligation if we mean to abide by it: so that if we depart from the rule, we break it; and whether the departure be little or much, it is still a violation of what we were bound to follow.

You will see, however, that although these principles belong to every rule, there is a great difference in the nature of the things themselves, and that it is a far more serious matter to violate some directions than others. A painter may add some inventions of his own as he copies a picture; or a scholar may make many variations from his model in writing, but these departures from what was taken as the rule, are much less important than would be the case, if the scholar should disobey his parents, or the painter break the laws of the state.

The great difference is that the one class of rulers directs us as to our moral conduct; that is as to what, in the sight of God, is right or wrong: the other class only directs us as to matters of art or education. We cannot tell whether a person is good or wicked, if we judge him by his penmanship or spelling. But if a man or child break any of the rules of moral conduct,—if he swear, steal, or lie, that violation proves his moral character to be evil.

Now the rule which is the subject of this book, is of the moral kind. Therefore, when we say it directs us, we mean that it is not like those which teach us how to act if we choose to do a certain thing, which we may do, or leave undone, according to our choice; but it directs us by showing what we *must* do, and how it is to be done. It is not like the hand-post which shows the way to several places, to any of which the traveller is at liberty to go; but it is like a person with authority pointing to a particular road and commanding us to take it.

CHAPTER II.

god's rule.

If you understand and reflect upon the illustrations, in the first chapter, of what a rule is, you will see that it is the very thing we need to direct us how we may glorify and enjoy God. For you already know that this is our chief end and duty; and that it is to be performed with the mind and heart. It is not like copying with the hand, or walking in a road, or learning lessons; but it is loving, serving, obeying, honouring, and delighting in God with the whole heart and soul.

But how can we do this without a rule to direct us? And who can give us such a rule? For consider what is necessary to be known before the direction can be given. Some one must be perfectly acquainted with the nature of God, or we should not know why He ought to be glorified, or how the enjoyment of Him could make us happy forever. The same one must also know what God wishes and requires us to do, or we should not know how to obey Him; and therefore we should not honour Him according to His will and authority. The same person must be perfectly acquainted with our nature, or the rule could not be suited to us. Without all this knowledge combined in some one being, it would be impossible to learn what would please God, what would make man happy, or how man could be directed as to both those objects.

There is no being who has such knowledge and wisdom but God himself. There is no other who perfectly knows Himself, or who perfectly knows man. There is no other who has authority to give moral laws to mankind. There is no other who has the power to bestow that blessedness, either in this world or in heaven, which is called the enjoyment of God.

If, then, we must have a rule, and if God be the only one who can give it, it is reasonable to suppose that He *has* given it. We cannot think that if God desired us to glorify Him, and were willing that we should be blessed for ever, He would omit to inform us of the way in which we were to do the one, and obtain the other. The question is, therefore, a very natural and proper one, and one that as accountable beings we are bound to ask, " What rule hath God given to direct us how we may glorify and enjoy Him?"

In order to answer this, we must look back to the very beginning of the history of our race.

When the first two persons were created, they were made, as you know, in the image of God. The soul of man and all its faculties were holy, and so much like the Divine nature, that man knew within himself what he ought to do to please his Maker and enjoy his favour. Besides this, he received instruction directly from God. The Lord is said to have spoken to Adam and Eve, and directed them as to their duty. So the rule which was given for the direction of the first of our race was a holy heart, and such instructions as God saw fit to give to them from time to time.

When they sinned, and so fell from the estate in which they were created, the heart of man ceased from that moment to be holy. But as to Adam, he still continued to know what he had once learned of his duty to God. He knew God. He had conscience and memory; and the rule, which he had received in his state of innocence, was his rule yet. The only change was in man's disposition and ability to follow it. The descendants of Adam received the same rule, but, being born with a corrupted nature, they did not perceive its excellence as their parent had when he was perfectly holy. It was as if Adam had received directions from heaven plainly written, but which men, by their own sin and folly, had so blotted and torn that they were no longer so distinct as when they were first given. Still, however, the character and will of God were known by his works, and by men's consciences; and He continued to speak to them in various ways. And when we come to the times of Abraham, Isaac, and Jacob, we find that the Lord revealed his will very often and plainly, and even condescended to make covenants with mankind, promising to bless the obedient and save the believing. He caused those covenants to include their infant children and families, so as to provide for the instruction of the people, from one generation to another, in the knowledge of the way in which they ought to go.

Thus, from Adam to Moses—a space of about twenty-five hundred years—the rule which directed mankind how to glorify and enjoy God, was that which they received from the history and experience of former ages, the instruction which was handed down through families, the observance of sacrifices, and other ordinances of worship, and the revelations which were made to particular persons by visions, the ministry of angels, and in other ways.

So far there was no written rule. But when the Hebrews had been brought out of Egypt and were on their way to their own land, God called Moses to mount Sinai, and there gave him the Ten Commandments written, or engraved, upon tablets of stone.

These Commandments cannot be considered as a new rule, but as the putting in express words what had been the rule from the very beginning. It had always been sinful to worship idols, to steal, to take the Lord's name in vain, and to do any thing else which was afterwards forbidden in the ten commandments. It had always been the duty of men to remember the Sabbath-day, to keep it holy, for it was instituted on the very day after man was created. The first son of Adam knew he was a murderer, though he slew Abel many hundred years before the commandment "thou shalt not kill" was written. The rule of moral conduct, therefore, which was given in a particular form through Moses, was the same rule that the first two human beings observed when they were holy. It was in their hearts; it was now put in words. Thus you find that our Catechism teaches us that "the rule which God at first revealed to man, for his obedience, was the moral law:" and that the moral law was not first made known to Moses, but "is summarily comprehended" (that is, the substance of it was given) "in the ten commandments."

CHAPTER III.

THE WORD OF GOD IS CONTAINED IN THE SCRIPTURES.

AFTER the ten commandments had been recited to Moses, they were delivered to him "written with the finger of God" (Exodus xxxi. 18,) on two tables or slabs of stone. We do not know how this writing was done;

but we know that Moses brought the written stones in his hands from the mountain where he received them from God, and placed them in the ark or chest of the tabernacle, where they were preserved for many centuries.

As the word Scripture signifies what is written, and as it is not probable that Moses had yet composed any part of the history which afterwards formed the first five books of the Bible, the ten commandments may be called the first Holy Scripture. This was the beginning of that written rule which now fills the Bible. After Moses had placed the stones in the ark, he was led by the Holy Spirit to write, (or if he had begun it before, to finish,) the history and laws contained in the books of Genesis, Exodus, Leviticus, Numbers and Deuteronomy. After him, other persons were in like manner inspired; some to continue the history which he began, some to compose psalms and proverbs, some to record prophecies. After the coming of Christ, others were inspired to write the history of those days, and to prepare an account of the doctrines of Christianity, as we find them in the gospels, epistles, and other books of the New Testament. All these together are called the Scriptures of the Old and New Testaments, or the Holy Bible; that is, the Holy Book.

You now perceive how properly this Scripture is called the word of God. The Bible contains many of the very words which God has at different times spoken, and the

THE ONLY RULE OF FAITH. 19

whole of it is a message or communication from God to man. It is like a letter which one writes, or dictates for another to write in his name. Such a letter contains the words which he would use if he should speak, instead of employing a pen. It is in this sense that the Lord Jesus Christ is sometimes called the Word; (John i. 1. 14.) because " God who at sundry times, and in divers manners spake in time past unto the fathers by the prophets, hath in these last days *spoken unto us* by his Son." (Heb. i. 1, 2.) The words of the prophets, apostles, and of Christ, are the words of God. We must believe them as readily as if they were spoken in our hearing with the voice of God. We are as much bound to do what they command us as Moses was, who received the moral law from God; or as John and James were, who heard the words of Christ. And whatever they forbid us to do, it must be as sinful for us to do it, as if like Adam and Eve, we should eat of a tree which God himself had expressly forbidden us to taste.

The Holy Scripture of the Old and New Testament is contained in the following books.

THE OLD TESTAMENT.

Genesis.	Judges.	Chronicles I.
Exodus.	Ruth.	Chronicles II.
Leviticus.	Samuel I.	Ezra.
Numbers.	Samuel II.	Nehemiah.
Deuteronomy.	Kings I.	Esther.
Joshua.	Kings II.	Job.

Psalms.	Ezekiel.	Micah.
Proverbs.	Daniel.	Nahum.
Ecclesiastes.	Hosea.	Habakkuk.
The Song of Songs.	Joel.	Zephaniah.
Isaiah.	Amos.	Haggai.
Jeremiah.	Obadiah.	Zechariah.
Lamentations.	Jonah.	Malachi.

THE NEW TESTAMENT.

The Gospels according to	Corinthians II.	The Epistle to the Hebrews.
Matthew.	Galatians.	The Epistle of James.
Mark.	Ephesians.	
Luke.	Philippians.	
John.	Colossians.	The first and second Epistles of Peter.
The Acts of the Apostles.	Thessalonians I.	
	Thessalonians II.	The first, second and third Epistles of John.
Paul's Epistles to the Romans.	To Timothy I.	
	To Timothy II.	
Corinthians I.	To Titus.	The Epistle of Jude.
	To Philemon.	The Revelation.

From this list you at once see that the whole Bible was not written at one time, nor by one person. If you are disposed to ask how we know that these different books really contain the word of God, I think the proofs that I shall now mention will satisfy you on that point. Let me beg your attention to them.

One very simple reason for receiving the Bible as the word of God is, that there is no reason to doubt its being so. Every thing in it, and every thing we know about it, shows that it is what it professes to be. I will try to explain the force of this proof.

There is a book commonly called "The Confession of Faith," containing a statement of the principal truths of religion, first in chapters, and again in two catechisms. This whole book comes to us, professing to have been composed by an Assembly of more than a hundred ministers of the gospel, who began to meet for that purpose in the city of Westminster, England, as long ago as the year 1643. This book has been received and used as the Westminster Assembly's book, from that time until now. All the men who assisted in writing it are dead. All the persons who were in the world at the time it was written, are also dead. Few persons have ever seen the papers it contains, as they were first written, so as to know that they were in the handwriting of the members of that Assembly. All that most of us have seen is the printed book, in editions published in our own time.

But the person would be considered unreasonable who should pretend to doubt whether this is the book it professes to be. Every reasonable person would say, it is enough that we have the testimony of history, and the book itself brought down from one family to another, and from one age to another, without its ever having been lost, to convince us that it is the Westminster Assembly's Confession. It speaks for itself too. For it expresses the views which we know were held by the members of that Assembly, and the persons whom they represented. There is, in short, no reason to doubt its being what it appears to be, and every reason to believe it. And if we are not able to tell who, out of all the Assembly, wrote this or that chapter of the book, it makes no difference in our belief of its being their book. All we care about knowing is that the Assembly, as such, prepared, adopted and published it as their Confession of Faith: and it would be a strange thing if we should say, we will not believe it to be theirs, because we did not see them write it.

In like manner the English Bible that we use, was translated from the Hebrew and Greek more than two hundred and thirty years ago, by forty-seven persons; and their translation was first printed in the year 1607. This book has been printed thousands of times. No one living ever saw any of the translators. Very few could tell their names, or what part each translated. But the book and its history have come down to us together; there is no reason to doubt its being what it is declared to be; and if a man should say he did not believe it to be the translation made by order of King James the First, no one would think his doubts to be worthy of serious notice.

Now the original Bible—that is the Holy Scripture as first written in Hebrew and Greek—is indeed far older than our English translation of it, and than our Confession of Faith. But there are the same reasons for knowing that it is what it professes to be— the word of God—and that it was written by the persons and at the times mentioned in the several books, as far as they are mentioned at all; and that whether mentioned or not, they were written by inspired persons, and have been preserved as one revelation, from the time they were begun until this day. As the books of the Old Testament were prepared, one after another, by the Divine direction, they were carefully preserved by the Jews, until the book was completed by the last prophecy—that of Malachi. That whole Testament was then copied hundreds of times, for four hundred and fifty years, until the prediction of Malachi about John the Baptist was fulfilled by his birth. Then Christ came, taught, suffered, died, arose and ascended. The four evangelists, chosen and inspired by the Holy Ghost, wrote separate accounts of the history and instructions of Christ; and their books were added to the Bible. They belong to the Bible, because the coming of Christ was the fulfilment of the promises and types of the Old Testament, and because every sentence that Christ spoke, he spoke as the Word of God. The miracles and other events, and the persons spoken of in those four books, were more or less known by those who first read them. They were not contradicted by any competent judges of the truth. Their books were copied and circulated in every age and among many nations of different languages. When printing was invented, they were multiplied by thousands and millions of copies. In every age they have been carefully compared with the oldest copies in existence, and so have been preserved without any important alteration. These are the gospels of Matthew, Mark, Luke, and John, which we have in our own language. On these grounds, therefore, we might as well doubt the truth or authorship of any history of Rome, or England, or the United States, which we have on good authority, as to doubt the gospels.

Precisely the same things might be said of the book called "The Acts of the Apostles," the several Epistles and the Revelation of John, which make up the rest of the New Testament. They were composed by a few persons, in the course of sixty years after the death of Christ. They completed the history of Christ, and of the first methods of making his coming known to the world; they gave explanations of his doctrines and precepts; they furnished a prophecy of some great events which should take place in future times; and then the New Testament was finished and the Bible completed. All these books have come to us together from our ancestors. They have never been lost or forgotten. Who, then, can be so presumptuous as to doubt that the Bible is genuine and authentic;—that is, that it is actually what it professes to be, as to its source; and perfectly true in all that it reveals?

CHAPTER IV.

THE HOLY SCRIPTURES ARE THEIR OWN WITNESS.

We have seen that there is no more reason to doubt that the Scriptures are the word of God, than there is to doubt any other book that has come to us from former times, which has been as carefully preserved, as constantly known, and as much regarded by multitudes of people as the Bible. I wish you to have this fact impressed on your minds, because the language of infidels sometimes leads the young to imagine that there is no such evidence in favour of the Bible as there is for other ancient books. If you should hear or read such foolish opinions, I hope you already feel that your reason would reject them. For I am confident that you must perceive that the Holy Bible stands far more favourably in this respect, than any common book can do. You must feel assured that a book that has always been regarded as the Old Testament has been by the Jews, and as the whole Bible has been by Christians, would be preserved with the most religious care, and that these sacred writings come to us so directly, that we may almost say we hear God speaking to us in them as by the word of his mouth.

But all that has been so far said on this subject is the smallest part of the proof that the word of God is contained in the Scriptures of the Old and New Testament. The Bible is its own evidence. By this I mean that if it had come to us from ancient times, only as common books have come to us, every truly wise and religious person, after reading and examining it, would say it was a divine book. He would be convinced of this by such reasons as those I shall now mention.

He would see that though the volume was made up of different books, and evidently by persons who lived in various countries and at different periods of the world, it is one book in its doctrines and history; and especially, that its representations of the attributes and actions of God all agree. He would see, also, that the books, though separately written, not only do not contradict each other, but that they explain and fulfil each other in a way that the writers could not have accomplished by any management of their own.

There are many prophecies in the Old Testament. They were written and spoken, some of them one hundred, some five hundred, some eight hundred, and some sixteen hundred years before the events which they foretold came to pass. Many of these events seemed very unlikely to occur. Many of the predictions referred, not only to persons who were not then born, but to nations and empires which had not yet come into existence. Some of the matters foretold were of so singular a nature, that they could not be clearly understood until they actually took place; but when the events occurred, it was at once seen that they exactly fulfilled the prophecy. The predictions of the Messiah, for example, were numerous and plain. They began almost as soon as man fell, and from the time of Abraham became more and more distinct as prophecies, though they were yet obscure to the people of those times. Jacob said of the family of one of his sons, " The sceptre shall not depart from Judah, nor a lawgiver from between his feet, until Shiloh come; and unto him shall the gathering of the people be." At the moment when the dying patriarch spoke this, Judah, who stood by him, was only known as one of his sons, and his whole family consisted of three sons and two grandchildren. How unlikely it must then have appeared, that this little family should grow into a nation and have a sceptre, that is, a race of kings and lawgivers, and that they should continue to exist in some form as a nation, until the Messiah should appear, and then their power cease! But when we follow the history of that tribe for more than eighteen hundred years, we see the short prophecy unfolded by degrees, a line of kings reaching through centuries, and then lawgivers of different kinds, until the coming of Christ found them again without a sceptre and a lawgiver.

There are other prophecies of Christ, as well as of the Jews, which were more plain and particular than this. His birth-place, his character, his sufferings, his death, and many other facts were expressly mentioned by the prophets. The Jews had their writings in their possession, and read them in their synagogues every week. These were precisely fulfilled, and contrary to the wishes and expectations of the Jews themselves.

Now, as God alone knows what is to take place in the future, none but God could have spoken by these various prophets, and their fulfilment proves that their writings were his word; and that the writers of the Old and New Testaments could not have contrived to make the Bible by their own invention.

Another source of evidence to sustain the Scriptures as the word of God, is the miracles by which God gave testimony to those who, from time to time, spoke in his name. The miracles which were performed by the instrumentality of Moses, Joshua, Elijah, the apostles and others, and especially those performed by Christ himself, and those in connexion with his death and resurrection, could not have been accomplished without divine power. They were performed for the purpose of proving that those who showed them, were sent by God, and that what they said, in the name of God, was true. That these miracles were performed is as well established as the other events recorded in the Bible, which, as we have seen, there is no reason to doubt, and every reason to believe. They are proved by many witnesses; they are numerous enough to extend over the whole compass of the sacred history, and yet so various, and occurring at such intervals, as not to lose their miraculous character by becoming common : they are consistent with the divine character; they have, indeed, nothing about them to justify a doubt of their being what they are related to be ; and they are so connected with the whole frame of the Scriptures, that their testimony to them as the word of God, includes the whole volume. The nature of this testimony cannot be more plainly expressed than it is in the sacred writings, in such passages as the following : " If I do not the works of my Father, believe me not. But if I do, though ye believe not me, believe the works; that ye may know and believe that the Father is in me, and I in him." "Believe me for the very works' sake." "Jesus, of Nazareth, a man approved of God among you by miracles, and wonders, and signs, which God did by him in the midst of you, as ye yourselves also know." "When the centurion and they that were with him watching Jesus, saw the earthquake and those things that were done, they feared greatly, saying, Truly this was the Son of God." " Long time abode they," [the apostles] "speaking boldly in the Lord, which gave testimony unto the word of his grace, and granted signs and wonders to be done by their hands." " We ought to give the more earnest heed to the things which we have heard, for if the word spoken by angels was steadfast, and every transgression and disobedience received a just recompense of reward, how shall we escape if we neglect so great salvation, which at the first began to be spoken by the Lord, and was confirmed unto us by them that heard him, God also bearing them witness, both with signs and wonders, and with divers miracles, and gifts of the Holy Ghost, according to his own will?" (John x. 37, 38. xiv. 11. Acts ii. 22. Matt. xxvii. 54. Acts xiv. 3. Heb. ii. 1—4.)

If, therefore, these miracles attested the messages of those who performed them, the record of the miracles comes down to us, with the same messages, as part of the proof that what is written in the Scriptures is the word of God.

But there is a stronger kind of proof still that the Scriptures are the word of God. It consists in their character, and their influence, or power.

They are so holy and so wise; they give us such views of the nature and attributes of God; they show so much more knowledge of the human nature than even man ever has until he looks at himself in this book as in a mirror; they furnish such heavenly doctrines and precepts; they make known so wonderful and yet so simple a plan of salvation, that no one who sees their excellence in these respects, can doubt that they are from God.

And they are known and felt to have such a power to convince, persuade and convert men; to comfort and sustain those who believe; to change the course of men from evil to good, from corrupt to holy ways, that those who read them in a right spirit are as conscious of their being the word of God, as they are that the light of day comes from the sun, or that they know the effects of light and heat. Nothing but divine truth ever has affected or can affect the human heart in this manner; no other work has ever been found so suitable to man; and if other books produce similar effects, it is owing entirely to the divine truth they contain, which their authors have first learned from the Bible.

The proof of the heavenly origin of the Scriptures, and of their being in all points what they claim to be, might be greatly extended. Many volumes have been written on this subject, some of which it would be well for you to read, if you desire to study the matter more fully, and to admire the wonderful manner in which God has provided evidence enough to satisfy any reasonable mind, that it is Himself who speaks to us by the writers of the Scriptures. But I think that even the short sketch which the size of this volume admits, contains such arguments as none but a very blind, or very wicked mind can resist. And if any are willing to make the best experiment the case admits of, let them adopt the course pointed out by our blessed Lord when he said "If any man will do his will, he shall know of the doctrine, whether it be of God, or whether I speak of myself." (John vii. 17.)

CHAPTER V.

THE WORD OF GOD DIRECTS US.

We have now learned what a rule is, and what is God's rule. The conclusion to which we are brought is, that as the Holy Scriptures are the word of God, their use is to serve as a rule in directing us "how we may glorify and enjoy Him."

You will remember that we found various ways in which we may be directed by a rule: and that it is not necessary in all cases to have a person to command us by word or by writing, in order that we should understand what we have to do. Children know that their parents can direct them by a look, or nod, or by pointing with the finger, as plainly as by saying to them, go there, or do this, or do not so, or do like this.

So the Scriptures give us the word of God for our direction in many different ways. There are some commandments and precepts in which God says to us expressly, "Thou shalt," and "Thou shalt not" do such and such things. Every one will acknowledge at once that these are plain rules.

But it is important for us to notice that every portion of the Bible is, in some sense, a rule to direct us, as well as those which are in the form of laws.

Perhaps you think that the historical parts of the Old and New Testaments are only to be read to gratify our curiosity about former times. This is a great mistake, and one which ought to be corrected before we form the habit of reading any portion of the blessed word for our amusement, or simply to gain knowledge. One great intention of giving so many books of history in the Bible, is to teach us our duty by the example of others. We see plainly in those books the rule by which God directed nations and individuals at various times, and perceive that he dealt with them according as they obeyed or disregarded his will. We learn from them the disposition of God towards our race, and how he requires us to glorify and serve him. We see his holiness, goodness, justice, and faithfulness, and are thereby directed to love, fear, and trust him. We see that God notices the conduct of the humblest, as well as of the most exalted persons; that he is the God of individuals, and of nations; and thus learn to regard him as *our* God and Judge. We see that he punishes sin and rewards obedience, and are directed by this to avoid the example of the one class, and follow that of the other.

This is the use that the sacred writers themselves make, and teach us to make of the Scripture history. The eleventh chapter of the epistle to the Hebrews is filled with references to historical passages of the Old Testament. More than twenty persons are named in that one chapter, for the purpose of teaching us, by their example, what faith is, and to encourage us to imitate them. This is as much as to say to us—when you read the account of Abel, Enoch, Noah, Abraham, and others, in the books of Genesis, Exodus, Joshua, Judges, Samuel, Kings, Chronicles, Daniel, Jeremiah, (for all these are particularly referred to in the allusions of that chapter,) you are to think that their conduct in showing confidence in God, even in the severest trials, is to be the rule of directing your confidence.

In another chapter of the same epistle, the sins of the Israelites in the wilderness are spoken of, in connection with their punishment, to warn us against unbelief and disobedience. "Let us labour, therefore," says the apostle, "to enter into that rest, lest any man fall after the same example of unbelief." "Take heed, brethren, lest there be in any of you an evil heart of unbelief, in departing from the living God." "Harden not your hearts as in the provocation," (Heb. iv. 11; iii. 12; iii. 8.) Such are the lessons he would have us learn when we read the history of the Jews. And in his first epistle to the Corinthians he expresses his desire that they would not forget the overthrow which was suffered in the wilderness, by the multitude with whom God was not well pleased. "Now these things," he adds, "were our examples, to the intent we should not lust after evil things, as they also lusted." And after drawing other warnings from the same history, he says again, "Now all these things happened unto them for ensamples; and they are written for our admonition." (1 Cor. x. 1—11.)

In like manner the epistle of Jude puts us in remembrance of the destruction of Sodom and Gomorrah, and the cities about them, which, he says, "are set forth for an example," to the wicked and impenitent, (ver. 7.) The epistle of James says to us, "take the prophets who have spoken in the name of the Lord, for an example of suffering affliction, and of patience. Ye have heard of the patience of Job, and have seen the end of the Lord; that the Lord is very pitiful, and of tender mercy." (James v. 10. 11.)

The same thing is true of the history in the New Testament. The disciples, the persons who came to Christ for mercies for their bodies or souls, the cases of Ananias and Sapphira, of Saul, of Lydia, and the many others which are recorded in the gospels and in the Acts of the Apostles—all are given for our instruction, as well as for our information. And even Christ himself, besides his divine character as Mediator, is set forth in the Scriptures as "leaving us an example, that we should follow his steps" in the meekness, benevolence, and purity of his life on earth. (1 Peter ii. 21—24.)

But you may say that no such uses as these can now be made of those large portions of the books of Moses which describe the ceremonies and observances of the Jews. As these did not form part of the moral law, and were to cease upon the coming of the Messiah, you may be disposed to conclude that they form no part of the rule which is to direct us.

It is true that these directions do not bind us in the sense in which they were first given to the Jews. There is no longer a priesthood, nor an altar, nor a temple: for Christ fulfilled what these things showed was to take place when he came, and therefore they are to be retained no more. But on this very account they furnish an important rule to direct our faith in Christ. The sacrifices, and services of priests, and the secrecy of the most holy place, were intended to keep up the expectation of him who was to offer himself as an atonement, and who having then gone into the very presence of God, should, by his intercession, open the way to all who should come through the Mediator. Those writings are, therefore, of great value to us in enabling us to understand the gospel. For we can compare the services which were prophetical or *typical* (as they are called,) with their accomplishment in and by Christ, and thus see the plan of our salvation more distinctly. So important did this seem to the inspired writers, that besides the numerous allusions made to these ancient ceremonies in all parts of the New Testament, the principal object of the entire epistle to the Hebrews is to show how they were fulfilled in the death of Christ, and in the effects of his death. This fulfilment is one of the certain proofs that Jesus is the Messiah; and when we see how the types of the Old Testament service agree with the New Testament history, we have one of the best illustrations of the way of salvation. On these, and other accounts, the Levitical law is a valuable part of the rule to direct us in understanding and obeying the New Testament.

And if you should be disposed to pass over the *prophetical* books of the Old Testament, under the idea that they are of no use, because most of them have been fulfilled, I hope you will consider the proof that they must always remain a part of the rule of our faith and conduct. For they, too, help us to understand the attributes of God and the manner in which he regards believers and unbelievers. They show us how just, as well as merciful, God is, and how he has always executed his threatenings as well as his promises. And as many of them refer to Christ, and to the spread of the gospel, they are guides to teach us our duty to the Saviour and to the world; and their assurances of success are our strongest encouragement to persevere in doing all that we can to send the Bible to every creature.

Nor can we say even of the *poetical* portions of the Bible that they form no part of God's rule. There is not one of the hundred and fifty psalms that is not profitable to show us our duty, and to help us in performing it. They are full of doctrine and precepts, as well as of praises and petitions. And these very praises and petitions are among the best rules we can have to direct us as to the spirit and manner of glorifying and serving God. Many of them, also, are prophetical of Christ and of his kingdom, and cannot be separated from the New Testament without leaving us in ignorance of the meaning of some of the most important allusions in the gospels and epistles.

It is to be feared that some persons read, not only the Old Testament, as if it were no more than a curious book, but that they imagine that many parts of the New Testament apply to none but those to whom they were first addressed. They think that what Christ said to the Pharisees, or the Apostles, to the Jews and Gentiles, or what the epistles declare to the churches at Rome, Corinth, and elsewhere, belongs chiefly, if not altogether, to those persons and churches. When they read these portions, they are thinking only of the people who first heard or read them, and do not feel as if it was all intended to govern their own conduct. But the fact that God has caused the whole to be preserved; and that the nature of man and the requirements of God, and the way of salvation, and the divine truth are all unchangeable, proves to us, that what has been said at any time, to any persons under the gospel, must be true at all times; and should be used by every reader or hearer for his own benefit. Besides this, God has directed us to "search the Scriptures," and declared that "all Scripture is given by inspiration of God, and is profitable for doctrine, for reproof, for correction, for instruction in righteousness." (2 Tim. iii. 16.) Whatever sins are rebuked in the Scribes, or Sadducees, or any others whom Christ reproved, would equally provoke the divine displeasure, if they should be committed by us. Whatever duties were commended in, or required of, the Ephesians, Thessalonians, or others of the seven churches of Asia, or of any others to whom the Apostles wrote, are our duties in the same circumstances. We should no more dare to disobey the precepts given first to them, or violate their spirit, than if spoken directly to ourselves.

CHAPTER VI.

HOW THE SCRIPTURES DIRECT US.

If we are bound to follow a certain rule, or direction, we must know what the rule is, and that it is intended for us. Many persons who receive the Scriptures as sent to be the guide of all mankind, still suppose that it is not important to be acquainted with every part of them. It is to keep you from such an opinion that I have tried to show you, in the last chapter, in what manner every part of the word of God may be improved as *our* rule.

It is also seen by this, that the Divine directions are given to us in many other forms than that of positive commandment. If the Scriptures declare that God disapproves of certain conduct, it is the same thing as if he had expressly forbidden it. And if he commends certain actions or dispositions, it is as much our duty to make them our rule, as if he had commanded us to do, or to be like the persons he approves of. Whatever expresses the will of God; whatever makes us know the things that please or displease him, we are to be directed by.

Thus when Christ said, " Blessed are the poor in spirit—blessed are the meek—blessed are the pure in heart—blessed are the peace-makers," it is just as truly a rule requiring us to be poor in spirit, meek, pure in heart, and peace-making, as if he had said, " Thou shalt be poor in spirit—thou shalt be meek," &c. And when the Apostle Paul expresses the judgment of God in saying "the love of money is the root of all evil," (1 Tim. vi. 10,) it is as much a law forbidding us to love money, as if he had said, " thou shalt not love money." So when the Psalmist says of those whom God will bless and accept, that they walk uprightly and work righteousness, do no evil to their neighbours, and despise vile persons, (Psalm xv.) this is enough to teach us that it is our duty to resemble this character.

Our blessed Saviour taught many things by parables. They teach us the same truths which they taught the persons who heard them from his lips. It would be just as mistaken in us, therefore, as it would have been in them, if we should read the parables only as pleasant stories. Each parable is a law—is a rule to direct us in some duty. For example:—The parable of the prodigal son is a message to every sinner against God, directing him to repent, and return to his heavenly Father; and the course pursued by the young man in the parable is a direction how such a sinner may return. The parable of the good Samaritan gives us as a rule, that we should be humane to all persons in distress; and gives us also an example of the manner in which it may be carried into effect. The parable of the Pharisee and Publican forbids pride and commands humility, when we pray; and directs us by the good example of one of those men, and the bad example of the other, what we are to do, and what we are to avoid, at such times.

There are parts of the Scripture which are called *doctrinal:* being truths that are given in the form of teaching us what we are to believe, rather than commanding us what we are to do. These doctrines are the rules of our faith or belief; directing us what we are to receive as holy truth. But whatever is true binds us to act accordingly, and therefore every doctrine may be said to be a rule of conduct, as well as of belief. It is a a doctrine of Scripture, that there are three persons in the Godhead, and that these three are but one God. This is revealed to us as a truth; and though we cannot explain it, we are bound to believe it, on God's word, and we are also bound to worship God as Three in One; and to honour the Son and the Holy Spirit as divine, as well as the Father. It is revealed as a fact, that the Son came into the world, in the form of man, and was named Jesus. It is revealed as a doctrine that he came to make an atonement for all who repent and believe. It is our duty to believe both the fact and the doctrine; and it is no less our duty to obey them both; that is, to receive Christ as the atonement, by repenting and believing.

There is still another way in which the word of God directs us. It is by giving the knowledge of practices and regulations which were adopted by those whose course was directed and approved by the Lord. There are no formal rules in the New Testament, saying that there shall be such and such officers in the Christian church; or that they shall be chosen and ordained in a particular way. But we find that the apostles who were inspired men, and entrusted by Christ with the establishment of his church, chose certain persons whose duty it was to teach and govern, in matters relating to religion, and who are called by several titles, but all applied to the same office—such as Minister, Pastor, Overseer, Bishop, Elder, or Presbyter. We find also from the Scriptures, that this class of men ordained or set apart such others as were found proper persons, to the same office, and that the form of doing this was by prayer and laying their hands on them. This example is our rule. It was approved by Christ, or it would not have been suggested to, or adopted by the apostles. It is, therefore, right, that none should be acknowledged as possessing this office, unless they have been ordained by those who already hold it. And it is wrong, because contrary to Scripture, to say that there is a distinct officer called Bishop, who alone has the right to ordain ministers.

It also appears from the practice of the apostles, and from their writings, that the class of ministers just spoken of, were assisted in the care of the churches by persons who were united with them in the office of government, but not in that of preaching. These are also called Elders, and are believed to be those mentioned in one of the epistles of Paul, as " the elders that rule well," whilst the others are called those " who labour in the word and doctrine." If this be so, then we are bound, if the same circumstances require it, to have in the church, elders or ministers to preach; and other elders to assist in government.

It seems also to have been the design of the apostles, to have another class of men to take care of the poor, and collect and distribute money for charitable purposes. These are called Deacons, and are believed to have been first appointed when the poor Grecian widows were neglected in the times of poverty among the first Christians. (Acts vi.) This being the case, we may still employ officers of this kind where they are required; and it would be a departure from the rule of the Scriptures to make deacons as such, a class of preachers.

Let me give you another example of this kind of direction which we receive from the word of God. We find that as soon as God began to call a people together who were to be known as his church, and who were to observe ordinances and laws that should distinguish them from the unbelieving part of the world, he made it a principle that the infant children of his people should be united with their parents in the membership of the church. To keep up the recollection of this right of the little children, their parents were required to bring their sons, as soon as they were eight days old, to receive a mark. This began in the time of Abraham, four hundred and thirty years before the time of Moses. We see, therefore, that it has nothing to do with the ceremonies of the law given to him, and which were to pass away when Christ should come. If, then, we cannot find that Christ or the inspired teachers and writers of the New Testament, ever said or did any thing to change this principle, or take away this right, we are bound to regard it as still a part of the truth; and believers, as still permitted and expected to have their infant children marked as members of the church of

God. This change of principle we cannot find. But, on the contrary, we see that Christ took up little children and spoke of them as belonging to "the kingdom of heaven," in such a way as implies that he meant the visible church, which he sometimes called by that title. And we also find that when certain parents became Christians, who had been heathens, their families were received into membership at the same time with themselves. (Acts xvi. 14, 15, 33. 1 Cor. i. 16.) All this makes a rule for us.

We do find one change in the rule. It is in the manner of marking the members of the church, whether adults or infants. The ordinances that existed in Abraham's time, as well as those that were instituted in the time of Moses, had the mark of blood about them, to signify that the true atonement was, at a future time, to be made by blood. But the time of blood has gone by; and Christ, foreseeing this, provided new emblems to be used in the church. The passover was not only a celebration of the deliverance of the Jews from Egypt, but a type of the Redeemer, as "the lamb of God that taketh away the sin of the world." (John i. 29.) As a remembrance of the death of Christ it was to be continued; but instead of killing a lamb and eating it with bitter herbs, as was the manner of the old passover, bread and wine were to be used. So Christ made no change in the rights of those who, by their birth, belonged to the church as first instituted. He only changed the sign from blood to water, and appointed the members of the Christian church to be marked, when received into it, with water instead of blood. Here is our rule. Believers should bring their children, as was done for two thousand years, from Abraham to Christ; but now they must be baptized with water, for so the precept and example of Christ and his apostles direct us.

So as to the rule of the Lord's day. The Sabbath was instituted at the creation. It was observed on the seventh day of the week, because the world was made in six days, and the first Sabbath was the seventh day. But from and after the death of Christ, through the rest of the New Testament and down to our own day, we find the first day of the week used for the Sabbath, and called the Lord's day, celebrating both the creation and redemption of man. As this change was made under the sanction of Christ himself, and as it just as fully meets the requirement of the law of the Sabbath, as the keeping of the seventh day, the example becomes as good authority for keeping the first day, as if Christ had given us the direction for the change in his own words, or by his inspired apostles. As in the case of infant membership the principle was continued, but the sign altered, so here the Sabbath is retained, but the time changed.

Such directions as these about the ministry, church-government, infant-membership, the Lord's day, and other things that might be named, are given to us from the example and practice of those who acted under the authority of the Lord Jesus Christ, and who now teach us through their history and writings in the New Testament. We are bound to keep to this rule as far as we can discover it; provided we have no reason to believe that their practices in any matters, were only intended to last for a time. Of course, it is as wrong to enforce observances that are not warranted by the Bible, as to neglect those which it establishes. We have the warrant of infant-membership, and therefore of infant baptism; and we have the warrant for observing the Lord's supper: but we have neither precept nor example for any ceremonies such as those called confirmation, penance and extreme unction, which the Romanists call sacraments, as well as baptism and the Lord's supper.

The Levitical law gave the most particular directions as to the form of the tabernacle, its furniture and services, the dress of the priests and all observances belonging to the divine worship. That was done because the whole arrangement was ceremonial and typical. It was to last only until Christ should come. All those rites disappeared when he offered the true atonement. When he came, he introduced a plainer and more spiritual service. Some few forms were still used, but they were only such as were needed to give expression to the feelings of the heart, and to enable believers to acknowledge one another as members of the same church, and to conduct their religious solemnities with propriety. Nothing is prescribed, therefore, in the New Testament, as to the particular manner, order, or gestures of public worship, or the observance of the ordinances. The duty is required, but the form is not minutely defined. We are exhorted to pray, to pray sincerely and fervently, and to be always in a spirit of prayer; but there is no rule as to the words we shall utter, or the posture we must use. Believers are directed to be baptized, with their households, in the name of the Father, Son, and Holy Ghost, in token of their faith; but no command or rule is given which binds us as to the quantity or quality of water to be used in baptism, or the manner in which it is to be applied. They are directed to commemorate the Lord Jesus, by observing the supper which he instituted for that purpose, but there is no direction as to the quantity or quality of the bread and wine used for the supper. So of singing psalms and hymns, preaching, the time and order of worship, and other matters of the like kind enjoined by the precepts or examples of the New Testament—the duties are plainly required, but the manner of their performance, as to what is merely external, is left to the discretion and judgment of Christians, according to the variety of their circumstances at different ages, or in different places. And if the *Scriptures* give us no plain and binding examples on these points, we cannot suppose that Christians are to be bound by the practice of others at any time since the Bible was completed.

CHAPTER VII.

THE SCRIPTURES ARE THE ONLY RULE.

But you may be disposed to ask—are there no other ways, in addition to the book known by us as the Holy Scriptures, in which God has revealed to us rules for our direction? Has he given no other book, before or since? Will he give no other?

But although I make the supposition that you ask such questions, I think you must feel that it is not very reasonable to expect more than one written rule. We naturally think that if God gives men any directions, they would be contained in one book, so that they might have his whole will before them. For as God is unchangeable, his will must be so. Whatever is morally right or wrong, must be always right or wrong. There can be, therefore, no such alterations of the duty of mankind towards God, as to require new books of laws. And if God has appointed one way of salvation, it must be the same for all mankind, and forever the same. The Jews, under the Old Testament, had reason to expect new books to be added to the Scriptures from time to time, because so long as the great atonement was not made, their religious system was not complete. They needed Moses to write the ceremonial law; then the prophets to prepare the way for the Messiah, by describing who he was to be; then the evangelists to inform them of the fulfilment of Moses and the prophets; and then the apostles to explain the doctrines and enforce the duties of Christianity. When this was done, the work was complete. For what else was there to reveal? The person so long looked for had come. He had accomplished his work. He had instructed and sent forth his disciples. He had ascended to heaven, not to return until the end of the world. Mankind were to be judged by the law and the gospel as now finished. How, then, could any thing be expected to be added to what was already given?

Another reason that may convince us that it is unreasonable to look for any other rule, than the Scriptures, as we now have them is, that all mankind have the same nature. Widely scattered as they are over the earth, all have sprung from the same stock and are of one family. We speak different languages, and have different customs, but as to our bodies, minds and souls, all are formed according to a common nature.

This is the case, also, with our moral character and history. It was not Adam alone, but human nature that was tried in Eden. He as fairly represented mankind, as one tree, or one fruit represents the nature and qualities of every other tree or fruit of the same kind. He did as all of us would have done in the same circumstances; so that it may truly be said of every human being that ever existed or ever shall exist, that in this respect, as well as according to the terms of the covenant with Adam, they "sinned in him and fell with him."

Our sinfulness does not consist in our different ways of sinning, but in our sinful nature, however it may be carried out. Of course, when God gives rules to mankind, or provides a way of changing our nature, and forgiving our sins, what is needed for any one is needed for all. It can make no difference in these matters, whether we live in Arabia or in America; whether our time of living falls in the year of the world 50, or the year of our Saviour 5000. We are all of one blood, all sinners, all need the same direction, the same salvation, and of course but one rule.

Again: What is true as an event or fact, must be true everywhere and at all times. That God created the world in six days and instituted a Sabbath-day; that a deluge covered the earth in the time of Noah; that Jesus was born at Bethlehem, and was crucified near Jerusalem, are facts that cannot be changed. These things are true in all parts of the world, and will be true forever. They are recorded in the Scriptures, together with a great number of facts which are equally true. This one record is sufficient.

No one would think of demanding several books to make known precisely the same facts. And if the Bible contain all this history, then the instruction of the history, whether it be to warn or encourage us, must be the same everywhere. All persons, wherever or whenever they live, are taught by this record to worship the Creator, to follow the example of the faithful, to shun that of the wicked, and so on. These instructions are the *only rules* which can be found.

And whatever *doctrines* the Bible teaches must, in like manner, be always and in all places true. If so, what they teach must be believed; and what they require must be the duty of men to perform, without any exception. If God is infinite in his power and knowledge, and is present in all places; if Christ Jesus has come into the world that whosoever believes in him may be saved, these and all other truths which the Scriptures reveal, are as true in Africa as in Europe; as true now as they ever were. Each of all these doctrines in the Scripture is the *only* truth on the point, and therefore there is only one rule to be observed respecting them. They must be believed and followed. The only rule of God's infinite power, knowledge and presence, is that we should adore him for these attributes, and act as if we believed that he is everywhere, knows our conduct and thoughts, and is able to punish or protect us. The only rule of the doctrine about Christ, mentioned above, is that we believe in him. This was the truth and the rule for Paul and Nicodemus; they are the same for the Hottentots and for ourselves! So that all men being of the same origin and possessing the same nature, owing the same duties to God; all guilty of sin against him ; and all lying in one condition of guilt and helplessness, reason teaches us to expect no more than one rule to direct us how we may glorify God, or how we may, after sinning, enjoy his favour again. We also see that truth being in its nature unchangeable, it cannot be supposed that God would reveal more than one rule for the direction of our race.

Let me close this chapter with a short illustration, which may help you to understand and remember what you have just read.

Every country has its history, and its laws. Its history cannot be changed, if it be once truly written. If Columbus discovered America in 1492; if the United States became independent in 1776; if Washington was the first president; these statements can never be otherwise than true. All persons who have proof that they are true, are bound to believe them, and indeed cannot help believing them. This history, so proved, is the only rule to direct us in our belief.

Each of our states has its laws. Those who are regarded as citizens at all, are considered equal in the sight of the law. There is not a book of laws for one class, and another for a different class. What the law forbids one to do, it forbids to all. The laws are in one book. They make one rule for all. This we all admit to be no more than reasonable and just.

It would be contrary to such views if we should imagine that God being the Creator of all men, and all being in the same moral condition, he could give different statements of the history and condition of mankind; or alter the duties which grow out of that history and condition; or give different laws, and different ways of salvation to men. On such accounts we must conclude that if we find one rule, full, plain, and suitable to all, it is reasonably to be received as the 'only rule. Such a rule is the Scriptures.

CHAPTER VIII.

THE SCRIPTURES SHOW THAT THEY ARE THE ONLY RULE.

ANOTHER proof that the word of God, as contained in the Scriptures, is the only rule to direct us, we find in the very character and language of that holy book. Every thing in it has the appearance of being the only revelation which God intends to make to the world. It speaks to all men, every where. It is suitable to all nations, and all classes of people, as soon as they are able to read, or understand what is read. Its doctrines may be believed, and its duties practised as well in one country as in another. We might be convinced of this by our examination of the Scriptures. But it has been proved by facts. The Bible has been taken to the farthest parts of the earth. It has been taught to the most ignorant and the most savage; the most wicked and the most refined; and there are instances in abundance, in all these classes, to prove that the word of God is a sufficient and suitable rule for every one; and that as soon as any submit to it, they become humble and obedient, as the children of God, and have the same kind of faith and love towards God, through Christ.

Again, every thing in the Scriptures shows that they are complete. Nothing is said about other rules. No future revelation is promised after the New Testament closes. We find no deficiencies to be supplied by other books, to be used with the Bible. In it is the history of our race. In it are the divine commandments as to our whole duty to God, to our fellow-creatures, and to ourselves. In it is the gospel, revealing the only way of salvation. What could be added, unless God should change his will, or the way of salvation? But this is impossible; for as he is perfect in every respect, he cannot change his will, and he declares that there is but one method by which any one can be accepted. How, then, can we imagine a new, or another rule, besides that which we have in the Bible?

The language of the Bible, in speaking of

its revelations to man, forbids any other idea than that it is our only rule. When it refers to its own contents as "the law," "the testimony," "the gospel," "the Holy Scriptures," "the word," "the word of God," "the word of Christ," "the oracles of God," and other expressions of the kind, the very names exclude the supposition that the revelation which is thus described, is only a part of the direction which God has given for our belief and conduct. These Scriptures are spoken of by the inspired writers as sufficient for all the purposes for which man needs a revelation. One of them, after declaring that they are "able to make wise unto salvation," and that they are "profitable for doctrine, for reproof, for correction, for instruction in righteousness," adds that they were given " that the man of God may be perfect, thoroughly furnished unto all good works," (2 Tim. iii. 15–17.) If it be capable of producing this effect, through the blessing of God, it is all that is wanted, and all that is to be expected. And as if to assure us of this in the most solemn manner, that apostle who received the revelation of the truth directly from our Lord Jesus Christ, has written, "though we, or an angel from heaven, preach any other gospel unto you than that which we have preached unto you, let him be accursed. As we said before, so say I now again, if any man preach any other gospel unto you than that ye have received, let him be accursed." (Gal. i. 8, 9. 12.)

There is no other standard mentioned in the Scriptures by which mankind are to be finally judged, but the truth which they make known. We "shall be judged by the law in the day when God shall judge the secrets of men by Jesus Christ, according to my gospel." (Rom. ii. 12, 16.) And the same passage declares that even those who have sinned without having the written Scriptures, shall be judged by them as a standard of duty, because God has so enlightened them in other ways as to make them "show the work of the law written in their hearts; their conscience also bearing witness, and their thoughts the mean while accusing, or else excusing one another." (Rom. ii. 15.) In all such passages we find but one law of conduct for the trial of all men. If that law has been given in writing, it must be the only book from which we can learn the rule.

CHAPTER IX.

THE SCRIPTURES WARN US AGAINST OTHER RULES.

When the apostle Paul was writing his first epistle to the church of the Thessalonians, he remembered with what reverence they had listened to the message which God sent to them by him and Silas and Timothy; and declared to them "for this cause also thank we God without ceasing, because when ye received the word of God which ye heard of us, ye received it not as the word of men, but (as it is in truth) the word of God, which effectually worketh also in you that believe." (1 Thess. ii. 13.) Paul and his companions were then making known by preaching, that truth which is now given to us in the writings of the New Testament. They spoke under the direction of the Holy Spirit; and under the same direction the writers of the gospels, epistles, and the other books of the New Testament put down the word of God for the instruction of us and of all others who should live after those writers were taken from this life. Their work being complete, it cannot be altered. It can never be in the power of any man, or any number of men, to change the word of God. As God has given to us one book, and every thing in it and about it assures us that it is the only revelation we shall ever receive, and that it is the book by which we shall be judged, we are sure that it must stand by itself, above the power of men to add to it, or change it in the smallest particular.

It is supposed by many wise persons, that what the apostle John records at the close of his vision, called the Revelation, was intended to apply to the whole Bible, as well as to that one book. "I testify unto every man that heareth the words of the prophecy of this book, if any man shall add unto these things, God shall add unto him the plagues that are written in this book; and if any man shall take away from the words of the book of this prophecy, God shall take away his part out of the book of life, and out of the holy city, and from the things which are written in this book." (Rev. xxii. 18, 19.) These are the last words of the Divine testimony as given in the Holy Scriptures; and whether intended or not to apply to the whole volume, as well as to John's prophecy, they give us a solemn admonition of the danger of attempting to add to or take from any portion of the word of God.

But this is not the only passage in which we are warned on this subject. Throughout the New Testament are many admonitions against departing from the plain revelations of the Scriptures, many prophecies of attempts that should be made to lead men away from the word, and several accounts of such attempts having been begun even before the New Testament was completed. Our Lord often reproved the Pharisees for the ceremonies and rules which they had added to the Scripture of the Old Testament, which he said was "teaching for commandments the doctrines of men." (Matt. xv. 7; Mark vii. 7.) The apostle Paul admonished the Colossians in similar language, when they were in danger of being persuaded to keep certain ordinances or human inventions, such as keeping a variety of what are called "holy days," or teaching the "worshipping of angels," and "voluntary humility," (that is, an external pretence of humiliation, as by what is called penance.) He called these "the commandments and doctrines of men," "the traditions of men," "the rudiments of the world," and exhorted believers to avoid such institutions, even when their inventors professed to connect them with Christianity. He condemned the whole system as a mere "show;" and as founded in "will-worship," or a kind of worship which men had devised, instead of following the spiritual system which Christ taught. (Colossians ii. 6—23.)

So the same inspired writer charged Timothy to study the Scriptures and continue in the things which he had learned, and to preach the word; and to do this the more diligently because the apostle knew that the time would come when men should turn away their ears from the truth and be turned unto fables. (2 Tim. iii. iv.) And at another time he put the same young minister on his guard against those who should introduce "doctrines of devils," such as "forbidding to marry, and commanding to abstain from meats." And again the Epistle to the Hebrews calls upon Christians to follow the faith of those who had spoken to them the word of God, and not to be carried about with divers and strange doctrines. (Heb. xiii. 7—9.)

Notwithstanding these warnings, and many others of the same kind, which are given in the Holy Scriptures, men have persevered in fulfilling the very predictions which should have taught them better. Some have added other things to the written word; some have put their own inventions in the place of the word; some have taught that we must have human authority to sanction and explain the word of God. These, and all other ways of leading men's minds from the Scriptures, as the sufficient guide, do as much as deny that the word of God, as contained in them, is *the only rule.*

It will be proper for us to consider some of these false rules. This is the more important because there has not been for many ages so much done to persuade men to depart from the only rule, as at this time. It is very necessary that our children and youth should hear and understand the warnings of the inspired writers against such opinions as would by their subtilty corrupt their minds from the simplicity that is in Christ. (2 Cor. xi. 3.) And there is no better way of doing this than by having them faithfully instructed in those right views of the authority of the Scripture, which, as well as their fundamental doctrines, may be called "the first principles of the oracles of God." (Heb. v. 12.)

———◆———

CHAPTER X.

OTHER RULES;—THE APOCRYPHA.

You will sometimes find bound in the same volume with the Scriptures of the Old and

New Testament, and between the two, several books which are not on the list of the sacred writings given in our third chapter. The names of these books are as follows:

Esdras; in two books.
Tobit.
Judith.
Additions to the book of Esther.
The Wisdom of Solomon.
The Wisdom of Jesus, the son of Sirach, or Ecclesiasticus.
Baruch.
The Song of the Three Holy Children.
The history of Susannah.
The history of the destruction of Bel and the Dragon.
The prayer of Manasses, king of Judah.
Maccabees; in two books.

This collection is called *The Apocrypha,* to distinguish it from the genuine Scriptures. Most of the books profess to treat of portions of the history of the Jews not so fully given in the Old Testament. Others are imitations of the book of Proverbs. Neither their authors, nor their precise date are known, but there is great reason to conclude that they were composed by Jews, at different periods, but not further back than two hundred years before the birth of Christ.

That the Apocrypha forms no part of the word of God is proved by the same standard as that which proves the genuineness and authenticity of the true Scriptures. As there is every thing in the genuine books themselves, and in the history of their origin, reception, and preservation, to establish their claims, and no just reason can be found to doubt their character, so the apocryphal books have no testimony which can lead us to think that they are inspired. They do not profess to be the work of inspiration: and so far as they are true, either in history or in doctrine, they cannot, on that account claim a divine origin, any more than the works of Josephus, which, though highly valuable, are but the production of a human mind. The apocryphal books have nothing in them or about them to induce us to attribute them to any higher source than common authors: and if they had never been printed with the Holy Scriptures, no one would have had reason to suppose that they had any connexion with them.

On the contrary there are many proofs that they cannot be inspired. One of these proofs, and all-sufficient in itself is, that the Apocrypha is full of assertions that contradict the true Bible, and contradict its own statements in other parts. For example, the book which takes the name of Solomon quotes from the prophecies of Isaiah, who wrote several centuries after Solomon lived. (Wisdom v. 18; xiii. 11—17.) In the first book of Maccabees, Antiochus Epiphanes is said to have died of remorse and grief in Babylon; in the second book, his death is spoken of again twice, and in the one place he is said to have been killed by priests in a Persian temple, and in the other to have perished miserably in a strange country among the mountains. (1 Macc. vi. 4—16; 2 Macc. i. 13—16; ix. 28.)

Then, the miracles and other events narrated in many of these books are so foolish and absurd, that any intelligent child would at once see the difference in this respect, between them and the wonderful instances of divine power recorded in the true Bible. The stories of the Apocrypha would encourage the most silly superstitions which the weak-minded have ever indulged, whereas the miracles of the Scriptures furnish nothing but what is consistent with the majesty of God and the right reason of man. To give a single example of this:—An angel is represented as offering himself as a guide to young Tobias on a long journey. He is said to be Raphael, "one of the seven holy angels, which present the prayers of the saints, and which go in and out before the glory of the Holy One." Yet this angel introduces himself to Tobias, with a falsehood, declaring that he is "Azarias, the son of Ananias the great," one of his brethren. (Tobit v. 12; xii. 15.) When they came to the river Tigris, the angel directed Tobias to open a fish, and take the heart, liver and gall, assuring him that the smoke of the burning heart or liver would drive out demons, or evil spirits, and that the gall would cure blindness. (Tobit vi.) How perfectly unlike the manner in which Elijah, Christ, or the apostles spoke and acted, when they showed mighty signs and wonders! But this is only a small specimen of the absurdities of the apocryphal writings, and the sins which they encourage by their fables.

Thus these books prove their own want of inspiration, as the true Scriptures prove their own divine origin. Besides this evidence against them, there are other testimonies of great weight; such as the fact that they are not found in the Hebrew language, in which the Old Testament is written, and to which part of the Bible they would belong if genuine. The Jews never received them as part of their sacred volume. And they are not to be found on the lists of the sacred writings, that are given by several authors in the early centuries of the Christian era.

The manner in which they have reached the place they occupy in some copies of the Bible is this. At first they were regarded only as all other human productions are. They were esteemed for what was true in their history, and good in their moral precepts. In the fourth century extracts from them began to be read in the churches on this account. As the Bible existed at that time only in manuscripts, and was not in the hands of many except the learned, the people could not at once distinguish between the inspired and the apocryphal portions that were read; and in the course of time the two would become more and more confounded together, even by the clergy. When (in the fourth century,) the learned Jerome published the Latin translation of the Bible, called the Vulgate, he inserted the Apocrypha; not because he considered it to be part of the word of God, but for convenience of reference to its illustrations of the Bible. This unfortunate step naturally tended to strengthen the mistaken notion of its character, and the impression increased during the ignorance of the dark ages, until the Roman Catholic Council, which met at Trent, in Italy, in the sixteenth century, decreed that these books should be thenceforth considered as part of the Holy Scriptures.

The Church of England, though expressly disowning the Apocrypha, as forming any part of the sacred canon, yet allows it to be read "for example of life and instruction of manners." (Article vi.) But, unhappily, it directs certain portions of these books to be read in the services of public worship. On this account it has continued to be printed with some of the larger copies of the Bible in our language. This is the reason why we find these uninspired writings in many of the editions of the Scriptures we use; and being divided into chapters and verses, like the Scriptures, they are the more likely to deceive the hasty reader. But they should never have any such connexion with the word of God as to be mistaken for a part of our only rule.

CHAPTER XI.

THE KORAN.—THE SHASTRES.—SWEDENBORG'S BOOKS, ETC.

About the year of our Lord 640, an Arabian, named Mohammed, formed the design of introducing a new religion. His principal object seems to have been to raise himself to a situation of authority and power over his countrymen; and as the best means of doing this, he determined to try to unite them in one religious belief, and to attach them to himself as a prophet of God. As the Arabians were divided into idolaters, Jews and Christians, he could not expect to bring them to agree in the Holy Scriptures as the foundation of their faith. He therefore declared that he was appointed to correct and finish the revelations that had been given through Moses, David, and Christ, and to require men, even by force, to acknowledge him as a prophet.

The account which he gave of his pretended inspiration was, that an angel was sent to him from heaven, at different times during a space of twenty-three years, communicating to him what he was to make known to the world. These revelations Mohammed afterwards dictated to a secretary who wrote them down, and they were at last published as one book, called the Koran. This book, according to his declaration, was to take the place of the Bible, and he persuaded or compelled all those who were under his power, to receive it as their only rule of belief and of duty. He was so successful in this, chiefly by the power of his armies, that the Koran has been so acknowledged by whole nations ever since his time.

But when you inquire for the evidences of the inspiration of this book, you can find nothing but Mohammed's own word to sustain it. He did not pretend to perform miracles. No one saw or heard the angel from whom he professed to obtain the revelation; and there was nothing in his own life or character which can give us any reason to account him a holy man.

If we examine the book itself, it has no marks whatever of its being any thing more than a human composition. It contains so many contradictions, that Mohammed was obliged to account for them by saying that the latest revelation was to be taken as the true one, instead of such as it contradicted; as if the divine mind could change, or commit mistakes! Whilst it copies and imitates many passages of the Bible, it contains many others which, if true, make the Bible false. The few examples of fine composition which it contains, are either taken from the Scriptures, or are inferior to similar expressions to be found there.* And, above all, whilst

---

* As one of the shortest examples of this, I copy from the second chapter of the Koran, (entitled *The Cow,*) a passage which is so much admired by the Mohamme-

there are in the Koran many moral precepts and religious doctrines, which are consistent with the divine attributes, they are mixed with so much sensuality and absurdity, that no one who has proper ideas of the holiness of God himself, and the spiritual purity which alone can please Him, can for a moment, believe such writings came from his inspiration. They not only tend to encourage licentiousness in this life, but scarcely give any higher description of heaven than as a place of bodily indulgence.

We find, therefore, that the proofs of this imposture are so plain, and the book itself so inconsistent with every proper conception of the character of God, that no intelligent and candid mind can imagine that the Koran has any thing to do with our rule of faith and conduct.

Another pretence of a divine revelation, still more ancient, is received by millions in

---

dans for its sublimity, that they recite it in their prayers, and sometimes carry it about them engraved on a precious stone.

"God! there is no God but He; the living, the self-subsisting; neither slumber nor sleep seizeth him; to him belongeth whatsoever is in heaven and on earth. Who is he that can intercede with him, but through his good pleasure? He knoweth that which is past, and that which is to come unto them, and they shall not comprehend any thing of his knowledge, but so far as he pleaseth."

True and beautiful as this is, the young reader can hardly fail to notice that the sense, and nearly the words, of every expression are taken from the Bible. (See Jer. x. 10. Psalm cxxi. 4. 1 Chron. xxix. 11. Isaiah xlvi. 9, 10. Psalm cxxxix. &c.)

India and elsewhere. It is called *Shastres*, or when spoken of by their separate books, *Vedas*, extending to a number of volumes, in prose and poetry. The history of the origin or authorship of these books is not known, as that of the Koran is. They are written in a language that has been known to Europeans, only within a few ages; and as they were kept by the Brahmins, or priests, as a sacred treasure, (which one large class of the Hindoos are not allowed so much as to see or hear,) they were not the subject of much inquiry by strangers. These books teach that there are three hundred and thirty-three millions of gods; and their account of the creation of the world, and of the history and character of their principal deities, is too absurd and wicked to impose on the mind of any intelligent child. These books profess to give not only religious truth, but to make known the principles of various sciences, such as astronomy and geography. And as these statements are proved to be false by our own knowledge, this of itself is enough to show that they cannot be a divine revelation. For example, these books declare that the earth is flat and not round; that the changes of the moon are the effects of the curse of an idol; and that eclipses are produced by serpents swallowing the sun or moon. Hundreds of such things, and far more ridiculous and absurd, are contained in the Vedas. If these are known to be false, and yet are part of a pretended revelation, the whole of which must stand or fall together, then we know that however ancient the books may be, they can have no claim to be a rule for our belief or our duty. The Bible is still older than the Vedas; and older than the Hindoos themselves; yet no discoveries of science, nor advancement of learning have found any error in its statements: and all that infidels have tried to do, in order to disprove the age of the earth, the period occupied in its creation, or its astronomical allusions, has only tended to confirm their truth.

About an hundred years ago there was in Sweden, a man named Swedenborg, who set up pretensions very much like those of Mohammed, excepting that he did not appear to aspire to any station of temporal authority. He declared that for twenty-seven years he received revelations from heaven, and was permitted to converse with angels. He wrote many volumes, in which he professed to make known what he had learned in this manner. His writings pretend to make a clearer revelation than the Bible, and to supply some doctrines which were omitted in the holy volume, which, however, Swedenborg admitted to be inspired. But the whole course of Swedenborg's history and writings proves him to have been either deluded by his imagination, or a wilful impostor. His teachings often contradict the Scriptures, and endeavour to give a sense to them which cannot be reconciled with their evident meaning. Indeed it is part of his doctrine that the Scriptures have three different senses, called the celestial, the spiritual, and the natural; and that the secret of their interpretation according to this mode, was revealed to himself, after it had been lost from the time of Job. Among the obvious contradictions of the plain statements of the Bible is his assertion that the last judgment took place in the year 1757, and that from that date, the new church founded by him, and predicted in the Apocalypse as "the New Jerusalem," began its existence.

If the principle I have endeavoured to prove be correct, namely that the Holy Scriptures are complete and were never intended to be altered or explained by new revelations, then the writings of Swedenborg, like those of Mohammed, are condemned on that ground. As they deny some of the most essential doctrines of the gospel, such as the atonement, *this* proves them to be an imposture. And besides all this, there was no evidence in the life of Swedenborg, and no such marks of heavenly wisdom or knowledge in his books, as to support his claims to have received divine direction in writing them.

I should not have thought fit so much as to mention, in addition to these examples of works that have been invented to deprive the Bible of its claim to be the only rule, a volume published in our own country within a few years, if it were not for the fact, that many persons have been deluded into the belief that it is inspired. I refer to what is called the book of Mormon. The history of this book, the bad character of the men who fabricated the story of its discovery, the ignorance, folly and blasphemy of its contents, are easily ascertained by any one who chooses to take the trouble of inquiring. The Hindoo Shasters can claim a venerable antiquity; the Koran, and the works of Swedenborg, with all their absurdities, manifest the talents of their writers; but there is nothing in the book of Mormon to redeem it from the contempt of an intelligent mind, much less of a mind that has any idea of the wisdom and holiness of God. That thousands have been the victims of this miserable imposition, should warn us of the danger of departing in any degree from the only rule, and of the duty of having our minds established in the evidence of the truth. We are already admonished by the Scriptures, and the success of the impostures we have been considering is a proof of the inspiration of the assurance, that if we suffer ourselves to be deceived by "lying wonders," and receive not "the love of the truth," we may expect to be given up to "strong delusion," so as to "believe a lie." (2 Thess. ii. 9—11.)

CHAPTER XII.

INWARD LIGHT.—HUMAN REASON, ETC.

The books and systems we have now considered as among the human inventions which would persuade us to abandon the only rule, are those which pretend to have no connexion with Christianity, or if any, of such a kind as to make the Scriptures inferior to the new revelations. But it is not only against Pagan idolatry, and artful forgeries, that we must be on our guard. There are some opinions held, even by those who profess to receive the Bible as inspired, which, if true, would greatly diminish its claims as the sole directory of our belief and practice. I shall mention some of the most common of these opinions.

It is held by the more orthodox portion of the society of Friends, that the Scriptures "are not to be esteemed the principal ground of all truth and knowledge, nor yet the adequate primary rule of faith and manners. Yet because they give a true and faithful testimony of the first foundation, they are and may be esteemed a *secondary rule*, subordinate to the Spirit, from which they have all their excellence and certainty."* If by

---

* Quoted from Barclay's Apology in "The Ancient Testimony of the Religious Society of Friends; revived and given forth by the Yearly Meeting held in Philadelphia, 1843."

this language nothing more were meant than that we need the influence of the Holy Spirit to make us understand and feel the power of the written word, this is what the Scriptures themselves teach. As our Catechism states that if the word ever becomes effectual to our salvation, we must "attend thereunto with diligence, preparation, and prayer, receive it with faith and love, lay it up in our hearts, and practise it in our lives," so it declares at the same time that "the Spirit of God maketh" the reading or hearing of the word the means of "convincing and converting sinners, and of building them up in holiness and comfort through faith unto salvation." But the truth, as given in the Scriptures, is always represented in the Bible, as the first source of light, and instruction. It is the instrument which the Holy Spirit uses for this purpose. It is "the sword of the Spirit." It is that which, according to the Psalmist, converts the soul, makes the simple wise, rejoices the heart, and enlightens the eyes. (Psal. xix.) Accordingly it becomes us to search the Scriptures that we may know the truth, and at the same time to pray that the Holy Spirit may enable us to understand, feel and obey it. But if we believe there is what the Friends call an "inward light," separate from the revealed word, and which is to be regarded as superior to the Scriptures, we are in danger of looking for private suggestions to our own minds, rather than consulting the complete and unchangeable standard of the holy book. This belief easily leads to great delusions and fanaticism. And there have sprung up, at various times, individuals and sects who have professed to receive direct communications from heaven, and on the belief or pretence of being thus taught by the Spirit, have acted in a manner most contrary to the precepts of the word. If we should trust to an inward light, we could not distinguish the effects of our own imagination from the revelation of truth. Our wise and merciful Creator, knowing this, has given us a sure word, a written testimony, containing all that is necessary for us to know and do, and by our disposition to believe and do which, we may determine whether or not we are led by the Spirit of God. It is, therefore, degrading to the only rule to say that it is "secondary."

Upon the same principles, we must warn the young against all opinions which set up any thing that the human mind alone originates, as any part of the rule to which we are to trust. Persons who claim to be wiser than others—calling themselves philosophers, freethinkers, rationalists, or whatever name they choose, are accustomed to speak, either as if they had no need of the Bible, or as if they meant to receive no more of it than they like; believing what pleases them, and rejecting what does not; and taking the word as their rule only so far as they can consent to it. Instead of coming to the Scriptures to get their knowledge and opinions from them, they take them up to judge of them by the opinions they have first made up for themselves. Hence they will receive some doctrines, and disbelieve others that are just as plainly revealed. They will approve of some precepts, and condemn the rest. Such persons generally profess to think that what we believe to be true and right, is therefore so, as to our responsibility, and that each one will be judged by his own belief, and treated accordingly. So that if a man denies that there is any state of future punishment, he need not fear that God will cause *him* to suffer it, even if there should be such a state, and he should be a sinner. And if one believes that the Sabbath is not to be kept holy, notwithstanding the commandment, then he may profane it and be excused, if it should prove, after all, to have been an unchangeable part of the moral law.

All such opinions are condemned by the fact, that they set aside the only rule. God has given us a written book, containing what we are to believe and do, and how we must be saved. If men were allowed to choose or reject, according to their wishes, there would be no use in having one rule; for every man would have to be judged by his own, and not God's. But it is in vain to expect that there will be more than one standard of judgment for those who have had the opportunity of knowing the Scriptures. And whatever proud man may say of his reason, his conscience, and his other faculties, he has light enough to show him that they are all given to be guided by the revealed truth, and that the revelation was not made to be controlled by *them*. It is on this account that the word so often teaches us that we must become as little children, in order to enter the kingdom of heaven; that we must depend upon the word for the strength and nourishment of our faith and piety, as infants depend upon milk; and that we must put no confidence in human wisdom or learning, but receive the plain truth just as God himself teaches it in his own inspired book.

CHAPTER XIII.

TRADITION.

By tradition in religion, is meant a divine rule which is not to be found in the Scriptures, but which is supposed to have been handed down from age to age, either by verbal report, or by uniform practice. Traditions, indeed, may be written or described in books; but when they are called verbal or oral, as distinguished from written, it is meant that they were not at first given to men in writing, or for the purpose of being immediately written, as was the case with the Scriptures. For example, the Jews, in connexion with the Old Testament, receive as equal in authority to it, a body of laws and doctrines which they imagine were given by the Lord to Moses, and though not written by him, were communicated to his successors, and by them to theirs, down to the second Christian century, when they were collected and written by a Rabbi Jehudah. This work is called the Mishna. The Jews also receive, as of Divine authority, another work, consisting of commentaries on the traditions of the Mishna, prepared from the third to the sixth century, and called the Gemara. The Mishna and and Gemara together form the Talmud, which may therefore be called the Jews' Bible of Tradition, in distinction from the written Bible. The Talmud contains much that is useful in illustrating the Old Testament, but is full of fables, and many of its professed explanations are so silly, as of themselves to prove the whole book to be no more than a human invention.

Tradition, as held by some Christian sects, is an opinion taken from this notion of the Jews, and is equally unfounded. It is, in substance, that the Bible alone is not full and plain enough to direct us; and that our understanding of the Holy Scriptures is to be controlled by the meaning which has been given to them by the consent of the church, and handed down from age to age; and that we are also to receive as binding, whatever doctrines or observances have come down to us by this long succession of agreement, even if no trace of the doctrine or practice is to be found in the Scriptures.

You perceive that either of these kinds of tradition would destroy the sole authority of the Scriptures as our rule. For if we may not take the Bible without first learning how certain persons, for a certain length of time, understood it, then their understanding of it is as much a rule as the word itself. And if we receive doctrines or ordinances, because they have come to us from ancient times, and hold them to be as binding as the Scriptures, though not to be found in them, then we take another rule besides the Bible. Yet this was the decision of the Council of Trent, only three hundred years since, which enjoined that not only the canonical books of the Old and New Testaments, and the spurious Apocrypha, but also " the unwritten traditions preserved in the Catholic church by uninterrupted succession," should be received with equal faith and veneration; and that no one should presume to hold the Scriptures in any other sense than that which the church has given, whose right alone it is to declare the meaning of the sacred word. According to this system, the interpretation of the Bible, or of the additions made to it by what is falsely called " the Church," is to be obtained from the decisions of the large councils held at different times to determine questions of doctrine and order, and from the writings of certain ancient writers called the Fathers, who are supposed to have obtained their knowledge from what the inspired apostles spoke, but did not write.

It was in consequence of the authority thus attached to tradition that many ceremonies of worship, religious ordinances, and even sacraments, grades and orders of ministry, and doctrines, unknown in and contrary to the scriptural revelation, were introduced from time to time. And, at length, these abuses reached such a height that the Bible became almost an unknown book. Tradition was the favourite guide. The fathers, and later writers, were the chief subjects of study. It was held to be easier and better to take the whole truth from them, with the advantage of their explanations and additional revelations, than to go to the Bible itself. It was in this state of things that Luther discovered the holy book in the library of the University of Erfurth, then retired to a monastery to study it, and left it to proclaim its blessed doctrines to the world.

We may say of all these opinions about tradition, that they bring no proof to sustain them, and that they are inconsistent with the uniform spirit of the Bible. That encourages all men to read and judge for themselves, using the best helps they can find to understand it, and humbly submitting their minds to the influence of the Holy Spirit. It says nothing of the privilege of reading or understanding the divine word being confined to a few. Nothing is hinted about a verbal tradition to accompany or follow the written book: and in regard to the difficulties of understanding it, its own sentiments are very justly expressed in our Confession of Faith, where it is said, "All things in Scripture are not alike plain in themselves, nor alike clear unto all; yet those things which are necessary to be known, believed and observed, for salvation, are so clearly propounded and opened in some place of Scripture or other, that not only the learned, but the unlearned, in a due use of the ordinary means, may attain unto a sufficient understanding of them." (Confession, ch. i. § 7.)

When the inspired writers use the word which is translated *tradition* in our Bible, they mean the messages and ordinances which they communicated by their preaching and epistles, and give no intimation that any persons were to be authorized to report, for the direction of future ages, what they had not put in writing. For an instance; the eleventh chapter of the first epistle to the Corinthians begins with commending those believers because they kept the "*ordinances*" as Paul had "*delivered*" them. And in the twenty-third verse of the same chapter, the apostle says, "I have received of the Lord, that which also I *delivered* unto you." Now the words *ordinances* and *delivered* in those verses, are those which signify *tradition* in the scriptural use of the word. The tradition, in this case, was the institution of the Lord's Supper. But the apostle had received this, as well as all other parts of the truth by inspiration, for the express purpose of instructing Christians in the duty of observing this ordinance. He did not leave this to be reported orally, but wrote it down in that very chapter, although it had already been announced by three of the evangelists. This explains what the apostle meant by tradition; and therefore we must understand it in this sense, when he says in the second epistle to the Thessalonians, "stand fast and hold *the traditions* which ye have been taught, whether by word or our epistle." (2 Thess. ii. 15.) That is, they were bound to receive all the truth he had taught them from God, whether in his preaching, conversation, or letters. This truth, so far as it was to be revealed to us, is furnished in his epistles and in the accounts given in the Acts of the Apostles, of what he said on different occasions. Of this truth we are certain. But no person was ever authorized to report what Paul was not directed by the Holy Spirit to write, and to send that report down from age to age to be received in connexion with his own writings.

When the Scriptures speak of any other traditions than these, it is only to condemn them. The Jews had mixed human inventions of this kind with the Old Testament. They undertook to say that the Bible did contain all the words of Moses, that were to direct the faith and conduct of men, and that what he had said verbally had been repeated from one to another till they had a large law besides that in his five books. But alluding to one of the practices introduced in this way, our Saviour charged the Jews with "making the commandment of God of no effect by their tradition," and again, with "transgressing the commandment by their tradition," and added, in a quotation from Isaiah (xxix. 13.) "in vain they do worship me, teaching for doctrines the commandments of men." (Matt. xv. 1—9.) "Beware," says the apostle to the Colossians, "lest any man spoil you through philosophy and vain deceit, after the tradition of men, after the rudiments of the world, and not after Christ." (Col. ii. 8.)

All tradition, therefore, *separate from the Bible*, is to be rejected, as having no authority in itself; because it brings no proof of inspiration; because the Scriptures are constantly represented, and are found to be complete and sufficient; and because no men, nor succession of men, however long or unanimously they may have held certain opinions, can establish any thing to be of Divine origin, that is not to be found in the Scriptures, in some of the ways considered in our sixth chapter.

CHAPTER XIV.

THE FATHERS.

One form of tradition which has drawn many minds from the Bible as the only rule, is that which professes to teach us some directions which the apostles intended us to receive by the writings of certain persons who heard their verbal instructions, or knew their religious customs. These persons are commonly called " The Apostolic Fathers." Their names are Barnabas, Clement, Hermas, Ignatius, and Polycarp ; and they are conjectured to have been connected with some of the apostles, either as fellow-labourers, pupils, or hearers. Then there are other ancient authors, also called Fathers, who did not live in the days of the apostles, but within three or four centuries from their time. Some of the principal of these are Justin, Irenæus, Tertullian, Origen, Cyprian, Eusebius, Athanasius, Chrysostom, Jerome, and Augustine.

But whatever might be the value and interest attached to such ancient Christian writers, yet even if all that is said of them be true, and we were sure that they lived when it is supposed they did, and wrote the books which now go by their names, their works would only stand in the same relation to the Holy Scriptures, as does the Jewish Talmud, already described, or their Targum, (which is an ancient commentary on the Old Testament,) or the writings of our own Christian commentators and biblical scholars. That is, we may use them to help us in studying the Bible; but we must try them all by the Bible. It is of great advantage to us in reading the Scriptures, to consult the opinions of good and learned writers, and to hear and read sermons and lectures; but we all know how to distinguish between the authority of the Scriptures, and that of their interpretation by men. If any thing stated in the Bible is altered, either by adding or taking away, or giving it a sense which it will not consistently bear, whatever writings or discourses do this, whether old or new, in apostolic times or in our own, must be as to those points rejected. A writing must bring the evidence of inspiration, or it cannot be received as forming any part of the only rule which God has given to direct us.

If therefore, we knew that the three authors, named Barnabas, Clement and Hermas, were the very persons named in the epistles of Paul as his "fellow labourers" or "brethren," (1 Cor. ix. 6. Phil. iv. 3. Rom. xvi. 4.) yet if their writings were not inserted in the sacred canon of the New Testament, they could have no authority as the word of God. They might be very excellent books to read; and might help us to understand the epistles of Paul ; but if they should enjoin as obligatory, matters whether of form or doctrine, which are not to be found in the Scriptures, or should give a sense to any thing in the epistles or gospels, different from that which a careful examination of the Scriptures themselves would give, we should be bound to reject them as in error, just as much as we should reject a book of the same character, written to-day.

But there is no such evidence as this to support any of the writings of the Fathers. There is not sufficient proof of their genuineness to warrant us in trusting to their being of the age ascribed to them, or to their being the works of the authors whose names they bear, or to their writers having ever seen or heard the apostles, or received any traditions from their times. So many forgeries and alterations have been detected, that doubt is thrown over the whole. And even if we take them to be genuine, we find that they differ from one another in opinion on important subjects, just as writers do now; and that they not only differ from each other, but that the same author differs from himself in his various writings.

Besides these and other reasons which might be given, proving that the Fathers have no higher claim upon our regard than any other merely human productions, it should be remembered that they themselves did not pretend, either to divine inspiration, or to any commission from the apostles to report explanations of, or additions to the written word.

As to the writings of the fathers, and certain observances which have come down to our day from the practices of former times, you will often hear it remarked that their antiquity recommends them to us. The minds of the young are apt to be imposed upon, not only by the pretended antiquity of what is really not very ancient, but by the argument that the older any opinion or practice is, which has prevailed in the church, the more likely it is to be true. But this argument is easily proved to be false. If there is a certain standard of truth, and we have that standard, every thing that does not agree with it must be wrong, however old it may be. The New Testament is the standard of what is true in the doctrines of the gospel. Any writings, out of the New Testament, even if they be as old as it is itself, that contradict what it teaches, or profess to teach what it omits, must be rejected as having no authority. The New Testament is older than the writings of the fathers; and they who love the true antiquity of Christianity will abide by the oldest, and the only inspired book. All that is taught by more modern writers than those of the Bible, so far as it is not to be found in the Bible, is a *novelty.*

Think of this illustration. Suppose that Demas, who was once a companion of Paul, but forsook him because he loved the world more than the truth, (2 Tim. iv. 10,) or Phygellus, or Hermogenes, who turned away from the same apostle in Asia, (2 Tim. i. 15,) or Hymeneus, or Alexander, who made shipwreck of their faith, (1 Tim. i. 19, 20,) had, any of them, written a book on Christianity, which had come down to our times, and we had received it without knowing it to be the work of an apostate. Here would have been a work by a contemporary and fellow-labourer of an apostle, and worthy, on this account, of being ranked with the five apostolic fathers. It might profess to give interpretations of the doctrines which its author had heard from Paul, or read in his epistles; or to furnish an account of the modes of worship or church-government which he used. Yet the whole of it may have been designed expressly to deceive and mislead those who should trust it as the testimony of one who saw and heard what he declared. And whether so designed or not, the moment the character of the author was known, every person who wished to learn the truth, would withdraw all confidence in it as a rule of belief. We see, then, that a book may be as ancient as the New Testament itself, and yet so far from its antiquity proving it to be worthy of our regard, it would only (in the case supposed,) prove it to be the less worthy of confidence.

CHAPTER XV.

THE CHURCH.

We have seen how uncertain a reliance any other book than the Bible is, on account of its mere *antiquity*. The same arguments prove that antiquity is no evidence for the authority or excellence of any opinion or practice which has come to us from the church of Christ in ancient times. That a doctrine or custom is old, does not prove it to be true or good. And as to any thing of this kind that is insisted upon as sanctioned by the consent of the church for many centuries, we know from the New Testament itself, as well as from other history, that we have no reason to trust in such testimony.

Before the writers of the New Testament died, and even before they began to write their epistles, there were many heresies and corruptions in the church. "I marvel," said Paul to the Galatians, "that ye are so soon removed from him that called you into the grace of Christ unto another gospel." (Gal. i. 6.) "I know this," he said to the elders of the Ephesian church, "that after my departing shall grievous wolves enter in among you, not sparing the flock: also of your own selves shall men arise, speaking perverse things, to draw away disciples after them." (Acts xx. 29, 30.) "There shall be false teachers among you," said Peter in one of his general epistles, " who privily shall bring in damnable heresies, and many shall follow their pernicious ways; by reason of whom the way of truth shall be evil spoken of." (2 Peter ii. 1, 2.) " Many false prophets are gone out into the world," said the apostle John. " Even now are there many antichrists, and they went out from us." (1 John ii. 18, 19; iv. 1.) The Corinthians are reproved for their abuses of the most sacred ordinances, and for great moral corruption, as well as for divisions, contentions and heresies. (1 Cor. i. 11; iii. 3; v. 1. 11; vi. 8; xi. 18—22.) And in the messages sent by Christ to the seven churches of Asia, they are charged with various departures from the truth and holiness of their professed faith, showing that great corruption and error were to be found among them, even before the end of the first Christian century, or the death of John. (Rev. ii. iii.)

Even, then, if other history did not inform us that these corruptions went on to increase and extend from century to century, the scriptural prophecies and statements would put us on our guard against trusting to what, in those early ages, might be believed or practised by Christian churches, beyond or besides what is to be found in the New Testament.

Besides this, reason would teach us to expect that the ignorance and superstition, the prejudices and customs of both Jews and Gentiles, would for a long time mix their influence, in some degree, with the simplicity of the gospel, and that there would be comparatively few who would fully perceive and follow the spirituality and simplicity of the new dispensation.

Yet there are those who will tell you that you must understand the Bible as it was understood in the first three or four centuries; and that if any religious customs have come from those ages, we are bound to observe them, because they must have been received from the apostles, and because the churches must have been purer, when they were so much nearer their times. If this rule were strictly adhered to, indeed, there would be but little innovation to be lamented. For so few genuine works of those centuries remain, and so few unscriptural or ex-scriptural customs can be traced that far, that we should not have much error, truly ancient, to contend with. But the corruptions of much later centuries are those which have increased, until they now form a system that requires a larger book than the New Testament to contain it. It is to these later times that are to be referred the titles, unknown to the New Testament as officers of the Christian church, of pope, cardinal, archbishop, priest, arch-deacon, dean, and numerous others now employed in unreformed or half-reformed churches. To these later days, too, belong the equally unscriptural inventions of five sacraments, in addition to the two instituted by Christ; of the invocation of saints; of saints' days; festivals and fasts; liturgies; the Lord's supper received kneeling from a priest, and before an altar; the mass; god-fathers, god-mothers and sponsors in baptism, and many other human institutions of a similar kind. That such things should gradually be incorporated into the services of worship and into the creeds of those who profess to receive Christianity as Christ taught it, is another warning to us of the danger of departing, ever so slightly, from the only rule as given in the written word of God. To see such inconsistent opinions and practices mixed with the simple truths of the gospel, should remind us of the caution of the apostle Paul against mingling with the gold, silver and precious stones, which alone become such a foundation as Jesus Christ has laid, the wood, hay and stubble, which are fit only to be burned. (1 Cor. iii. 11—15.) Yet such is the character of the inventions added by tradition.

Let me add one more illustration of the folly of trusting in any other antiquity than such as is in the New Testament. Suppose that eighteen hundred years hence it should become a question how the doctrines of Luther, Calvin, or president Edwards, were understood by those who received their writings as a just exposition of the Scriptures. Suppose, furthermore, that at that remote period, the religious opinions of Germany, Geneva, or New England, could be gathered only from the histories of the first, second and third centuries after those eminent men, respectively, lived—that is, about our own time in the nineteenth century. If this method of finding the truth should be employed, the inquirers at that time would conclude that Luther was a deist, and Calvin and Edwards Unitarians: because in our day these heresies abound in the very countries where the truth as they taught it, once flourished most extensively, and where it might be expected to be found still flourishing. Yet the doctrines of Neology and Socinianism, now professed by so many in those countries, are as opposite as can be to what those great men believed and taught. If the true state of their opinions would be ascertained, the only proper method would be to read and try to understand their own writings. In like manner, it is unsafe for us to take what any fathers, or any church professed to hold in the early centuries, as more likely to be true than our own understanding of the Holy Scriptures, simply because they lived so much nearer to the time when the Scriptures were written.

You must not allow yourselves, therefore, to be deceived by the assertion that there is any particular body of Christians called "the church," who either now or at any other time have had the authority to explain the Scriptures, or hand down institutions that are to be added to what the Scriptures reveal. By "the church," the Bible means all those persons who have been, or shall be saved, through the Lord Jesus Christ. The name is also given to those, who are joined together as believers, in any particular society, even though some of them may be hypocrites. In the former sense, the church is said to be invisible, because we do not know certainly who are the only true believers, and because it comprises all who have gone to heaven as well as those who are still on the earth. In the other sense, the church is said to be visible, because it exists as a society with officers and rulers, and ordinances, and can be seen. The Scriptures say nothing of any authority having been given to the church, in either of these meanings, to add to, alter, or establish the interpretation of, what they reveal. It has handed down *the truth;* but it has done so by handing down *the Bible.* This is the only real tradition of the church, and it is done simply by preserving, multiplying and scattering the sacred volume. This church is not confined to any one denomination, nor to any particular succession of ministers; but embraces all who truly receive and obey the word, truly acknowledge and follow Christ, and truly preach his gospel, being in an orderly manner ordained for that purpose. It is evident also, as a matter of fact and history, that there has never existed since the end of the Jewish dispensation, any one body that could be called "the church" as a body of believers, whose interpretation of the Scriptures could be ascertained and fixed. The gospel provides for no officers, or bodies of men, to do this. None such exist or have existed, that possess this authority. What is sometimes pretended to be the voice of "the church," is nothing more than the opinions of commentators on the Bible, who wrote on their own suggestion, just as men write books now; or the decisions of councils or conventions, where only a part of the Christian world was represented, and where questions were determined by the vote of the majority, each voting according to his own opinion, as men now vote in any kind of public meeting. No more authority belongs to these councils, than if several hundred ministers were now to meet in New York, and give their interpretation of the Scriptures.

It follows from the Bible being given as our only rule, that it is to be received by itself; and that no man or body of men may say that we must not pretend to understand it, without receiving some other book with it to explain it. It is right that a church should set down in order, what its members believe to be the doctrines taught in the Bible. This is done in our Confession of Faith and Catechisms; but we do not say that these are necessary to make the Scriptures intelligible. On the contrary the Confession itself says, "the infallible rule of interpretation of Scripture, is the Scripture itself; and therefore when there is a question about the true and full sense of any scripture, (which is not manifold, but one,) it may be searched and known by other places that speak more clearly." (Chap. i. § 10.)

It follows also, that the Bible should be read by all, and its meaning judged by all for themselves, with the best help they can procure in comparing the Scriptures, in hearing sermons, in consulting the works of those who have studied the word, and with constant prayer that the Holy Spirit would bless these means to their discovery of all that it is necessary for them to know. To forbid any to read the Scriptures; to restrict any as to the portions they may read; or to require them to believe as certain books or councils or churches believe, is a violation of the rights of conscience, and of the law of God.

CHAPTER XVI.

CONCLUSION.

"THE Holy Scriptures," said Paul, addressing one who had been taught them from his childhood, "are able to make thee wise unto salvation, through faith which is in Christ Jesus." (2 Tim. iii. 15.) *Salvation* is the great object for all sinners to seek after. The way of salvation is only to be learned from the *Scriptures*. In order to know the way aright, we must obtain *wisdom* from the Scriptures. The wisdom of this knowledge is to have *faith in Christ.* Here, then, are the four steps which may be said to lead from the condemnation of sin to the blessedness of peace with God:—The Scriptures—Wisdom—Faith—Salvation.

To prove to you that God speaks to us in the Scriptures, and that in them he has given us the only rule to direct us to eternal life and happiness, has been the object of the previous chapters. I hope that your mind, my young reader, has been convinced of these truths. But now let me solemnly remind you, that if you believe the Scriptures to contain the word of God, it is not enough to believe this to be so, nor is it enough to be acquainted with all that the Bible contains. Your knowledge must make you so wise as to convince you that you are a sinner, and that you can only be saved by Christ, and only by believing on him with your heart, and to lead you thus to believe, or it will be of no benefit to you. When the Scriptures are received "not as the word of men, but as the word of God," that is, taken and obeyed as the word of God ought to be, then it "effectually worketh in you that believe." (1 Thess. ii. 13.) It produces its proper effect in convincing its readers of their guilt, their danger, their helplessness in themselves, and of their only but all sufficient remedy. It brings them to repentance; it leads them to Christ; it makes them his humble and obedient disciples. This is the "effectual work" of the sacred truth, when the Holy Spirit makes it the means (as David wrote,) of "enlightening the eyes, making wise the simple, converting the soul, and rejoicing the heart." (Psal. xix. 7, 8.)

Would you not be pleased to have this effect produced on yourself by the Scriptures? Do you not feel that it *must* be your duty to read, study and hear the word of God, as that which concerns your own happiness and welfare more than any other truth in the world? It is a rule—God's rule—his rule for you—for your duty and for your salvation—the only rule, and can you be either wise or safe in neglecting it? It is given to you in love; it is meant for your good. It is the advice and instruction of a heavenly Father; of a Saviour who loved you so much as to die for you; of a blessed Spirit who is able and ready to make you holy. Can you find it in your heart to neglect such a proof of love and goodness? Remember, too, that if you are not made wise unto salvation by this truth, there is no other way of salvation. Christ is the only Saviour. Faith is the only means of being saved by him. The Scriptures are the only source of the wisdom that leads to faith. If we neglect the Scriptures, we have no wisdom. If we have no wisdom, we have no faith. If we have no faith, we have no Saviour. If we have no Saviour, we have no hope!

Many of my young readers have been taught the Scriptures from their childhood. Many of them have been carried by their parents to be received by baptism as heirs of that promise to the children of believers, which they will surely receive, if they will themselves live consistently with their baptism; that is, if the baptized children, when they can understand their duty to Christ, will receive him as their Saviour. Shall this knowledge and this privilege be in vain? Will you disown what has been done for you by your parents and the ministers of Christ? Will you not study and obey that very word which God has given to tell you of Christ and to make known the rule to direct you, how to glorify him and enjoy him for ever?

Hoping and praying that all our readers will be brought to a determination to use the Scriptures, I will close this book with a few directions how they should proceed in using the holy writings. And these rules apply not only to your own reading of the Bible, but to all the opportunities you have of hearing it explained and enforced in preaching: for the word, when truly preached, is of the same authority as when read.

I. Keep your minds in the firm persuasion that it is the word of God which you have in the Scriptures.

This is necessary to fix your *attention* in a proper manner on the truth. When Moses heard God speaking to him on the mount, during the forty days he spent there, he could not help being attentive. He knew it was the voice of God. You should have the same feeling when you use the Bible. It should seem to you as true and as important to be attended to, as if you heard the words coming from Christ, or from the lips of the sacred writers.

II. Feel your need of the Scriptures as a rule to direct you.

The Bible is useless to many, because they think that they have no necessity for it, or that they know it well enough already. Let it not be so with you. Think how little you know of God, or of yourself; how little you care about divine and heavenly things; and how unable you are of yourself to find out the truth, or to discover what you must believe or do. Reflect upon the nature of the Bible as described in the third answer of the Shorter Catechism: "The Scriptures principally teach what man is to believe concerning God, and what duty God requires of man." These two subjects are the highest and most important of all branches of knowledge. Without the Scriptures, we cannot receive any satisfactory instruction. Take them, therefore, as the more precious for their being the only source of such information, and realize that in them you are to find the words of eternal life.

III. Use the Scriptures with a proper sense of your dependence on God to make them useful to you.

You must use your mind in understanding, remembering and judging of what the Bible contains; but you cannot help feeling that you want more strength for this than your faculties alone give you; your memory, reason and perception are weak and uncertain. Above all, you will find that even when you seem to understand well enough, you do not feel as you think you ought to do, and as you would do if you *realized* what you read to be true. Perhaps you read of God, of heaven, of hell, of eternity, of the sufferings and death of Christ, with no more awe, or anxiety, or love, than you read the history of England, or the life of a distinguished man. But if God's Spirit helps you, you can feel as you ought to do, and be disposed to do what you ought to do, in reference to the great subjects of the Bible. This is part of the wisdom which God hath promised to give liberally to those who desire and ask for it. (James i. 5, 6.) You should feel as David did when he saw that it was his duty to do, as well as to know, the divine will. He said, "thou hast commanded us to keep thy precepts diligently. Oh that my ways were directed to keep thy statutes. Open thou mine eyes, that I may behold wondrous things out of thy law. Make me to understand the way of thy precepts. Strengthen thou me according to thy word. Teach me, O, Lord, the way of thy statutes. Give me understanding, and I shall keep thy law. Incline my heart unto thy testimonies. Teach me good judgment and knowledge. Let my heart be sound in thy statutes. Quicken me, O Lord, according to thy word. Hold thou me up and I shall be safe; and I will have respect to thy statutes continually. Order my steps in thy word." (Psalm cxix.) Let such petitions as these be in your heart and on your lips, when you read or hear the word.

IV. Be willing, whilst you read and pray, to be directed by the truth. Do not think that you have nothing more to do than to learn and pray. Resolve to believe and to follow the truth as you are taught it. Take up the Bible, as the captain of a vessel takes up the chart of his voyage. He does it, that he may direct his ship in the course there set down, and not for the pleasure or amusement of knowing what his course is, and then paying no attention to the dangers it warns him of, or the safest and shortest passage it lays down. He consults his chart *for the purpose* of following it. So do you take up the Bible, with the intention of directing your belief and your conduct by it at once and for ever. Make up your mind to do this, and pray for strength and wisdom to be added to your knowledge. Then,

V. Attend to the one great end of all the wisdom and direction you desire.

The object of the sea-captain is to reach a certain place. That place is the point or end at which he is aiming. To arrive at it safely and soon is the very reason why he is so attentive to every direction of the chart every hour of his voyage, although it may last for months. The end of faith is the salvation of our souls. (1 Peter i. 9.) The great inquiry that should be in our minds is, "What must I do to be saved?" Keep this before you, as the result to which you hope to come. Let it shape your inquiries, urge your diligence, and be the subject of your prayers.

VI. As one means of reaching this end, apply every thing in the Scriptures to your own case, so far as it teaches you what is the relation and character in which you stand to God.

When the Bible declares the sinfulness and deceitfulness of the heart, look at your own and see if you find this to be its condition. If you are not convinced at once, continue the examination of yourself by the truth. Consider God in his infinite perfections, as they are there revealed. Think of his holiness and goodness as displayed in his laws and words; his dealing with men and angels. Think of his claims upon us as our Creator and Father; and our duty as his creatures and children. You can imagine what Adam and Eve ought to have been, and to have continued to be, after they were placed in Eden, and surrounded with so many proofs of the divine goodness, and so much knowledge of what was pleasing to God. Ask yourself what reason there was to expect them to be holy, obedient and affectionate towards their Maker, that does not exist in your own case. Then look at your own character; your holiness, obedience and affection; your gratitude to God; your remembrance of him; your regard for him as "the Lord, YOUR God."

You cannot do this sincerely and honestly, without being persuaded that it is true you are a sinful and ungrateful child of your heavenly Father. When you are fully convinced of this, the next step, of course, is,

VII. To be sorry for your condition, and for the cause of it.

Can you do less? Have you offended God, and do you not regret it? Have you been unthankful and undutiful, and are you not ashamed of it? Have you discovered that you have been going away from God, and should you not at once wish to return to him? Does not a child, when sorry for offending a parent, desire to go to him and confess his fault? This is repentance. It is sorrow for having done wrong, and returning to God with confession of the wrong, and a purpose to sin no more. And as God has provided for the case of such as repent, and appointed a way by which they may return to him and be sure of forgiveness, the person who sincerely desires to be reconciled, will follow that way: it is,

VIII. Through faith in the Lord Jesus Christ.

Being the Son of God, he became man and by his righteousness in obeying the law and suffering its penalty in the place of sinners, he is "the way, the truth, and the life," to all true penitents. Go, then, to Christ in this character. Truly believe that he is what the Scriptures declare him to be; and believing, trust in him as *your* Saviour. Do not doubt that he is able to save them to the uttermost, that come unto God by him, (Heb. vii. 25;) that him that cometh to him, he will in no wise cast out. (John vi. 37.) Believe, therefore, that he is able and willing to save *you:* and that he will do this simply upon your trusting in him to do it, when you are sorry for your sins, are willing to forsake them, and desire to be a true Christian.

IX. Show your desire and purpose by professing your faith.

If you are in earnest, why should you wish to hide your repentance and faith? If you believe Christ and trust in him, why should you not acknowledge it? Are you ashamed of it? If you are not, then confess that you have seen the error of your former course, and are resolved to be a disciple of the Saviour. If you have been baptized as the child of a believing parent, go as soon as you are satisfied of the sincerity of your purpose, and ask for admission to the Lord's table. It was instituted as a means of acknowledging Christ, of remembering him, and of strengthening the faith of his disciples. Be not afraid to take your place among his people; for they do not go to the ordinances to profess their piety, or to hold themselves up as better than others, but to confess their sinfulness and acknowledge that their only hope is in the mercy of God for Christ's sake.

THE ONLY RULE OF FAITH.

Their feelings may be expressed in the words of our beautiful hymn:

> "My faith would lay her hand
> On that dear head of thine,
> While like a penitent I stand,
> And there confess my sin.
>
> "My soul looks back to see
> The burdens thou didst bear,
> When hanging on the cursed tree,
> And hopes her guilt was there."

In coming to the Lord's table, having been baptized in infancy, you acknowledge and confirm what was then done for you. You express your free consent to be what your parents knew you ought to be, a disciple of the Saviour. If you have not been so baptized, then before uniting with Christians at the table of the Lord, you should ask for baptism, that you may signify your confession of sin, your desire to be cleansed and forgiven, and your dependence on the blood of Christ, as applied through the Holy Spirit, for producing that effect. You will not expect the water to take away sin; but you will look to it, when used according to Christ's appointment, as the sign of what you hope and pray will be effected in your heart; and as a seal, to express your entering into that covenant or agreement, by which God engages to save those who believe, and by which the believer engages to trust and serve the Lord. And lastly,

X. You should continue to use the Scriptures as the means of your improvement until you leave this world.

The word of God is the rule to direct us to the eternal enjoyment of the presence of God. We must follow it, therefore, till we come to that chief end of our being. We shall need it every day "for doctrine, for reproof, for correction, for instruction in righteousness," that we may be "perfect," that is, complete in the various parts of our duty, and "thoroughly furnished unto all good works." (2 Tim. iii. 16, 17.) There is much to learn after we have become believers. We are then only just enlightened, and enabled to understand the Scriptures properly. We have then but just entered upon a course, at every step of which we need direction. We have just entered a school, knowing only the first elements of our future studies. But persevere in reading the Scriptures, in praying for understanding and strength, in believing what they teach, in doing what they require, and shunning what they forbid, and as sure as the promise of the Lord is true, so surely will he at length bring you to receive "the end of your faith, even the salvation of your souls." (1 Peter i. 9.)

THE END.

A COMPANION TITLE

THE CHIEF END OF MAN
An Exposition of the First Answer of the Shorter Catechism
by John Hall

In addition to the title you hold in your hand, Solid Ground is delighted to have also published the companion title by John Hall, **The Chief End of Man**, which is an exposition of the First Answer to the Shorter Catechism.

Q. WHAT IS THE CHIEF END OF MAN?
A. Man's Chief End is to glorify God and to enjoy Him forever

This little gem is full of instruction on the reason we are here and the way that we can live to the glory of God and the enjoyment of God. Parents and children, teachers and pupils, pastors and congregation alike will benefit from this wonderful book.

An introductory article by Benjamin Warfield on the Benefits of the Shorter Catechism adds to the value of this timely work.

SOLID GROUND CHRISTIAN BOOKS
10380 SW VILLAGE CENTER DRIVE, PMB 403
PORT ST LUCIE, FL 34987
www.solid-ground-books.com
mike.sgcb@gmail.com
205-587-4480

www.ingramcontent.com/pod-product-compliance
Lightning Source LLC
LaVergne TN
LVHW051658080426
835511LV00017B/2627